STOP KISSING FROGS

Prentice Hall LIFE

If life is what you make it, then making it better starts here.

What we learn today can change our lives tomorrow. It can change our goals or change our minds; open up new opportunities or simply inspire us to make a difference. That's why we have created a new breed of books that do more to help you make more of *your* life.

Whether you want more confidence or less stress, a new skill or a different perspective, we've designed *Prentice Hall Life* books to help you to make a change for the better. Together with our authors we share a commitment to bring you the brightest ideas and best ways to manage your life, work and wealth.

In these pages we hope you'll find the ideas you need for the life *you* want. Go on, help yourself.

It's what you make it

* * *

Stop Kissing Frogs

How to avoid Mr Wrong and find Mr Right

MADELEINE LOWE

Prentice Hall Life
is an imprint of

Harlow, England • London • New York • Boston • San Francisco • Toronto
Sydney • Tokyo • Singapore • Hong Kong • Seoul • Taipei • New Delhi
Cape Town • Madrid • Mexico City • Amsterdam • Munich • Paris • Milan

PEARSON EDUCATION LIMITED

Edinburgh Gate
Harlow CM20 2JE
Tel: +44 (0)1279 623623
Fax: +44 (0)1279 431059
Website: www.pearsoned.co.uk

First published in Great Britain in 2010

ISBN: 978–0–273–73052–1

British Library Cataloguing-in-Publication Data
A catalogue record for this book is available from the British Library

Library of Congress Cataloging-in-Publication Data
Lowe, Madeleine.
   Stop kissing frogs : how to avoid Mr Wrong and find Mr Right / Madeleine Lowe.
      p. cm.
   ISBN 978-0-273-73052-1 (pbk.)
   1. Man-woman relationships. 2. Mate selection. I. Title.
   HQ801.L677 2010
   646.7'7–dc22
                              2009043563

10 9 8 7 6 5 4 3 2 1
13 12 11 10 09

Text design by Julie Martin
Cartoons by Bill Piggins
Typeset in Ehrhardt MT Std 12/16pt by 3
Printed and bound in Great Britain by Clays Ltd., Bungay, Suffolk

The Publisher's policy is to use paper manufactured from sustainable forests.

This book is dedicated to Rachel. Thanks for dragging me out of more ponds than I care to remember.

CONTENTS

...

ACKNOWLEDGEMENTS

•••

A huge thank you goes to my wonderful and very funny editor, Ellie, who's been a great source of support and frog stories – I particularly enjoyed the tale about sewing the prawns into the curtains. Many thanks also go to all the girls who were more than willing to dish the dirt on their dating horrors – without you there wouldn't have been a book.

Extract from 'This Be The Verse' taken from *Collected Poems* by Philip Larkin © The Estate of Philip Larkin and reproduced by permission of Faber and Faber Ltd.

INTRODUCTION

...

I JUST DON'T GET IT.

I HAD A FAIRYTALE upbringing. My parents loved me. My friends liked me. Even my brother tolerated me (apart from the time I stabbed him with a picnic fork after he made Barbie do unspeakable things to Action Man). Overall, I enjoyed a childhood stuffed with love, encouragement and laughter. So far, so good.

So how is it that I turned into an adult who made such hideous choices about personal relationships? How can I have been someone who felt blindingly confident about work and friendships and yet ended up with such low expectations about love?

And I'm not the only one. Why is it that so many bright, attractive and sensible women seem to go for such utter toads? There are thousands upon thousands of smashing, eligible blokes out there and yet most of us seem to manage to miss them. It may be true that you have to kiss a few frogs before you find Prince Charming, but do we really have to go through a pondful before finding happiness?

I have a daughter. She's only very little at the moment, but before I know it she'll be bringing home boyfriends and making tentative steps into the grown-up world of relationships. The worst thing I could do is to spend her childhood bitching about blokes. Not only is this an incredibly negative way to talk about relationships but it's also wholly inaccurate. Most men are great. In fact, pretty much all the men I know, through family and friends, are utterly lovely. This book isn't a cheap opportunity for some male-bashing. It's the exact opposite. It's a plea to women to stop picking out the few rotten apples.

So this book is partly a way of consolidating what I've learnt about loving relationships ... and the not-so-loving ones. It's also a chance to take a light-hearted look at some of the common mistakes we girls make on a depressingly regular basis. And it's a serious attempt to see through the myths about men and women and analyse what truly makes a good mate.

The language of make-believe is often used to describe relationships – Prince Charmings, dreams coming true, dragon-like mothers-in-law, knights in shining armour and damsels in distress. This idealisation of love and relationships is great for bedtime stories but the whole point of this book is to inject a bit of reality. It's going to take more than braiding your hair and swooning a lot to find someone who'll make you happy in the long run. And Prince Charming is going to need more than a well-honed six-pack and a flashy steed to win fair maiden. After reading this book, you may decide that you actually don't want a Prince Charming and prefer being single (I hear there's an excellent book called *The Kama Sutra for One*, although you might need to be fairly bendy to get any value for money).

Looking back, I dated some stinkers. And it seemed as if I kept repeating the same mistakes time and time again. In looking at *why* I kept making such an arse of myself, I've discovered lessons about how women prepare themselves for the world of love, what kind of traps we can fall into, and how many of us don't recognise Prince Charming even when he's staring us in the face.

One of the best bits about this book is that it includes experiences from other women. I didn't need to look very far to find willing subjects keen to spill the beans about horrible boyfriends and happy endings. The search for Mr Right is rarely a straightforward process, and it's true that we learn from our mistakes, but hopefully their experiences will ring true. Only by understanding patterns in poor relationships can we avoid pitfalls in our own.

On a happier note, after kissing what seems like a knob of toads (you can thank my editor for knowing the collective noun), four years ago I finally met the man I want to spend the rest of my life with. We met when my little girl was only six months old. I was recently separated from my then husband and definitely *not* looking for another bloke. What I did need, however, was a gardener and he showed up, face smeared with mud and wielding a chainsaw. The rest is history. Meeting the love of your life via the Yellow Pages might not be the most conventional route but it was certainly quick, free and I got my ivy trimmed in the process.

We're now married and he wouldn't mind me saying that he's not my 'type' in lots of ways, and I'm not his. We come from completely different backgrounds. We have completely different interests. His refusal to get a haircut annoys me on an almost daily basis. And yet it works. Brilliantly. I've finally found someone who lets me be myself. Who loves me regardless. Who I feel completely at ease with. It just goes to show that love comes in many guises. Above all, it has shown me that true love has nothing to do with manipulation, game-playing or trickery. Prince Charming is out there, girls, but first you've got to stop hanging around ponds.

1

Chapter One

IDENTIFYING A FROG AT FIFTY PACES

...

Uh oh, you've done it again. Just when you think you've bagged yourself a handsome prince, he emits a loud croak and hops back into his pond.

It can be difficult to spot a frog when you're fishing through rose-tinted glasses. When we're desperate for a relationship, we lose all sense of reason. Whether it's loneliness, boredom or you've simply had enough of dry-humping the furniture, a boyfriend can suddenly seem like the answer to your prayers.

So what happens when your bloke isn't all he's cracked up to be? Is being in a relationship, however bad, better than being on your own? Don't you believe it. Desperation, distraction or lust are never good reasons to start a romance and you can end up picking an absolute stinker. There are thousands upon thousands of fantastic, sexy, articulate men out there, but you have to recognise a sinner before you can pick a winner.

• TEN TYPES OF GUY YOU SHOULDN'T • TOUCH WITH A BARGEPOLE

I almost feel guilty writing this chapter. Not because I don't think these guys exist but because they don't make up the majority. They're the exception to the rule, but boy do we ladies know how to find them.

The following ten frogs are, of course, shameless generali-sations. You might recognise elements of a past boyfriend's character or perhaps you were really unlucky and your bloke fitted more than one category (one friend has dated six of the ten types ... all in one guy. If there's a medal for crap dating, she takes the gold ... or should it be brown?) Either way, it's important to keep your eyes open for the following telltale signs ...

• MR LIAR LIAR PANTS ON FIRE •

I used to tell horrible whoppers when I was little. I remember cutting a hole in the bathroom curtains and telling my dad my brother had done it. Whilst he was banned from watching *Star Trek* for a week, I felt little more than a quick frisson of guilt before returning to some top-level fibbing.

As a mature and fairly sensible woman, I now recognise that bare-faced lying is wrong. It doesn't stop me from telling the odd white lie but at least I'm decent enough to feel bad about it. So why is it that some blokes never seem to progress from playground porkies, even when they're in grown-up relationships? I'm talking, of course, about Mr Liar Liar Pants on Fire. Deception may seem small-fry in comparison to verbal or physical poundings, but there's something intensely sinister about a bloke who can't or won't tell the truth.

Past conquests, current lives, jobs, exes, money, qualifications, feelings, experiences – Mr Liar Liar can fabricate fantasies about pretty much anything. Some lies are huge – denying you've got kids is a major one – some lies are tiny – saying you've seen a film which you haven't – but the impulse is the same. So what drives a liar and why are they a dating disaster?

Liars lie for lots of different reasons. Some people are unlucky enough to be genetically predisposed to porkies. Men with certain learning disabilities, for example, or brain injuries are prone to pathologically lie but let's face it, they're rare. And they've got an excuse.

Your average bloke lies for social reasons. Guys who come from dysfunctional or chaotic backgrounds often fib to make their reality more palatable. They lie from an early age to avoid harsh or inconsistent punishment from their parents (the 'It wasn't me!' lie) or as a coping mechanism to try and move on from a troubled past. Sometimes men lie because they don't want to hurt other people's feelings. Others do it to evade responsibility or blame.

Lies can also be a form of denial, when we can't face the truth of our lives – perhaps that we're not as successful, good-looking, rich or popular as we'd hoped. Sometimes lies are used to instil fear or to control people. Sometimes they make us more interesting or attractive than we really are. Most of all, Mr Liar Liar fibs to conceal his real self – usually because he thinks he's inadequate – or he wants to gain an advantage over you. Neither of which you need, thank you very much.

So why is an emotional fraudster such a dating dud? What's a few lies between lovers? It's one thing to tell a few fibs now and again or to embellish the odd story – I once tried to get a gorgeous graduate to snog me by saying that I had a PhD in Primatology (that's monkey studies to you and me) and it worked, hee hee. But dating someone who habitually lies is fraught with danger. If he lies about something, and you don't find out, it's a problem because you are essentially being deprived of the tools to make a good decision. If you don't know the full facts, you can never make an accurate assessment about an issue.

Let me give you an example – your bloke lies and says he's always used a condom with ex-partners. On the basis of that information, you believe that he's unlikely to have an STD and you sleep with him without using a condom. The lie has not only tricked you into making a decision that you wouldn't ordinarily have made, but there's also a good chance you'll pick up something nasty along the way.

If he lies and *you find out*, it's no better. Not only do you feel deceived and manipulated but you're also pissed off that he didn't feel you deserved the truth. If it goes on long enough, dating Mr Liar Liar will leave you doubting your own judgement, untrusting, and constantly cynical about other people's motives.

66 I dated Mr Liar Liar in my late teens, when I was too young to know better. I met him whilst I was working at the local theatre – he was an actor and constantly bragged about all the famous shows he'd been in, how much he earned and all his celebrity 'mates'. After every evening performance, he'd always be the first to the bar, showering everyone with drinks and picking up the tab. I assumed he must have lots of money to be able to spend such a lot on booze for all the cast and crew. We dated for only a few months but he'd never let me see where he lived – he always met me at work – but he promised that one day he'd show me the 'amazing apartment' he was renting. When I finally found out his address, I thought I'd surprise him with a visit. When I turned up, not only was his amazing flat a horrible, smelly bedsit, but he was sitting in the dark, smoking a fag. He didn't even seem that shocked to see me – all his defences went down and he plaintively asked if I had 50p for the electricity meter. So much for his glamorous lifestyle. 99

Adele

• MR CONTROLLING •

I can be bossy – just ask my husband. I never fail to be surprised and delighted when someone actually does what I tell them. Fortunately, friends and family cheerfully ignore me most of the time and rarely indulge my controlling tendencies. And so it should be. People thrive in relationships where there's give and take in equal measure. It doesn't do either partner any good when one person has more control.

So let's get one thing straight from the start. There is absolutely nothing sexy, romantic or wonderfully old-fashioned about being dominated. Life with a controlling man is demeaning, damaging and potentially deadly. Whether it's constant put-downs or being pushy in the bedroom, emotional control comes in many guises. Checking up on what you're doing or who you're with, constantly criticising or making cruel jokes, laying down the law about work, sex, home and money, and even isolating you from family and friends – these are all classic signs that you're dating Mr Controlling.

Controllers think of themselves as perfectionists. No-one could possibly be as wonderful as they are. They quickly get irritated by other people's weaknesses or mistakes, however tiny, and this makes them short-tempered and intolerant. Like a tyrannical toddler, they generally get their own way, often resorting to guilt, threats, bullying, shouting or physical violence. Women who've had relationships with controlling men also know that it can be difficult to escape. Men who control their partners, with or without their fists, often carry on trying to dominate their ex-partners even after the relationship is long over.

Women who've had relationships with controlling men also know that it can be difficult to escape.

Ironically, domineering men can be very charming. At the early stages of a relationship, Mr Controlling often starts out being chivalrous – picking up the tab, whisking you away, ordering for both of you, surprising you with clothes and jewellery. There's no decision-making to be done – he's thought of everything. But don't be fooled. These are all subtle forms of control and before you know it, Mr Controlling will want to do all your thinking for you whether you like it or not.

Controllers seem compassionate at times, a contradiction which makes many women struggle to leave. Fits of fury are often followed with protracted periods of tears, guilt and regret. He didn't mean to do it. You drove him to it. If only he didn't care so much about you. Next time will be different. Your confidence and independence are slowly eroded by months of alternating anger and affection – you may even start to believe that you deserve nothing more.

So what motivates Mr Controlling? Sometimes it's no other reason than the sense of pleasure which comes from having power over another human being. More often, however, the underlying goal of a controller is to take command of a situation he feels threatened by. Fear drives his desire to control. Fear of ridicule. Fear of failure. Fear of being alone. Fear of being controlled by someone else. He's too afraid to construct a healthy relationship, inhabited by equals, because a partner who is unwilling to be controlled or possessed may leave at any time. In reality he controls nothing apart from you.

Mr Controlling will often shroud himself with tradition. He expects servitude, weakness, loyalty, dependence and utter devotion from his partner. He does this because he's desperate for a stable, predictable existence. But life is capricious – the more erratic his outside life becomes, the more inflexible and demanding he becomes with you. If things go tits up at work, for example, you can bet you'll be the first to know.

Make no mistake, this is not real love. I have two all-time favourite quotes. The first is "Never eat more than you can lift" but sadly Miss Piggy's wise words are not relevant here. The second is from psychologist Carl Jung and sums up Mr Controlling to a tee: "Where love rules, there is no will to power, and where power predominates, there love is lacking." Ain't that the truth.

66 I was married to a controller for 15 years. On his good days he was incredibly romantic – he'd write poetry, shower me with gifts, tell me he loved me dozens of times a day. The only problem was that he was also insanely jealous. When we weren't together he would ring me and ask where I was, who I was with. Whatever I said, he always seemed to twist it around to me being unfaithful.

Every other bloke was a threat – even people on TV. It sounds almost funny now but he became convinced that I fancied Take That and would turn them off if they came on the screen. I can also remember suggesting that I go see a film with a mutual male friend of ours – he flipped and punched a window out. Violent outburst weren't uncommon – although never towards me – but he'd always be smashing things in frustration. He was also great at sulking and name calling – slag, whore, tease. Horrible sexual insults.

From the outside our relationship looked perfect and my friends used to say they envied our marriage. He always behaved impeccably in public, but all the time I knew he was watching me. It was only when we were alone that he'd let rip. We finally got divorced a few years ago. I now understand that he was really insecure, always terrified that people would abandon him, including me. Maybe that's why he tried so hard to keep me on a tight leash. ""

Jenny

No-one should have to endure physical, emotional, psychological, financial or sexual abuse. Domestic violence is a crime. If you need help leaving an abusive relationship, or know someone who does, REFUGE has a 24-hour confidential, free helpline on 0808 2000 247 which provides support, information and a listening ear.

• MR PLAYER •

Have you ever noticed that men who constantly boast that they 'just lurvvve women' tend to be the ones who treat you like dog poo? Womanisers, two-timers, lotharios, love rats, lady killers – call them what you want, but personally I find that there's nothing more tedious than a player.

He might have all the right moves, but Mr Player falls way short when it comes to making any real emotional connection. For the brief moment that you're the apple of his eye, you feel like a million dollars. The sweet nothings, the irresistible kisses, the grand gestures and nights of wild passion – it's like a whirlwind holiday romance without the squits. But while you're browsing through wedding magazines picking out tiaras, there's every chance he's got his eye on his next conquest. In fact, he's probably already shagging her too.

So what's behind this serial bonking? Some men may not be up to the challenge or responsibility of a long-term relationship and use womanising as a protective layer. They feel safe as long as no-one gets too close. Fine… but do you really want to be dating an emotional cripple? Scientists have also discovered an infidelity gene, believe it or not, a 'love rat' segment of DNA which stops men's brains from releasing a bonding chemical called vasopressin, so they can't form lasting relationships. Call me cynical, but do we think it might have been a bloke who made that particular scientific breakthrough?

More often than not, however, it's nothing more complicated than Mr Player enjoying the thrill of sleeping with multiple women and getting away with it. And why not? Womanisers can be fun and exciting. They're having the time of their lives. If you want nothing more than a no-strings seeing-to, then by all means date a love rat, but don't expect him to change. If he's enjoying himself, he'll find no reason to stop, even if you've fallen head over heels. As long as he's being upfront about his infidelities, you only have yourself to blame if you stay. If, however, he's presented himself as Mr Right whilst simultaneously schtupping half the street and your sister, you've got cause to complain. He's crossed over into the Mr Liar Liar category, so you're effectively getting two frogs for the price of one.

So what are the signs to watch out for? While your gut instinct is probably your greatest ally, if your bloke takes longer to get ready in the bathroom than you do, constantly flirts with other women including your close pals, rarely introduces you to his friends or family, behaves very secretively on the phone or around his computer, and always calls you instead of you calling him, there's a good chance there's something fishy going on. Remember, ladies, if it looks like a rat and smells like a rat ... it's probably a rat.

" I met Alex at work. He completely wooed me. He relentlessly pursued me for eight months, constantly texting and flirting outrageously with me in front of all the other staff. He was gorgeous and I fancied the pants off him – my tummy would do flips every time I saw him. I resisted for so long because we worked together but I finally gave in.

From that moment on everything changed. He stopped talking to me at work, insisted we keep our relationship hush-hush and he flirted with my colleagues, whilst suddenly I became invisible. Whilst it drove me crazy, I soon realised I was smitten and desperate to tell all my friends at work. Finally I let it slip and was taken to one side and told that Alex was actually seeing another member of staff. I refused to believe it until I caught them shagging in the disabled loos at the Christmas party. Then I saw him for what he was – a complete player. The other woman didn't know about me and I didn't know about her – we'd both been told by Alex to keep our relationships secret. No wonder.

Three years later I'm happily married. And Alex? He's still playing. "

Natalie

• MR EEYORE •

I'm going to get into big trouble for this category. It must seem really harsh to say "Don't date someone with depression", but let me explain where I'm coming from.

I've both been depressed and lived with someone with depression. I know people who've survived mental illness and those who are still living with it. It sucks. Depression can strike at any age, any time and can affect absolutely anybody. If you are in a serious relationship and you or your partner develops depression, I'm not saying you should leave. They're going to need you now more than ever and it's vital you work at managing the illness together.

I also know people who have made a success of a relationship with someone suffering from depression. In fact, their illness can be a great source of creativity, emotional maturity and warmth. Depression also covers a wide range of conditions, so it's not fair to compare someone with mild, intermittent depression to a person who struggles with manic depression on a daily basis. Couples who have made it work make a point of talking openly about the problem and how it affects the relationship. Developing strategies for how you ride the rough times is vital for both of you.

But this is a book about dating, so let's get real. There's a world of difference between dealing with depression when it strikes a previously healthy relationship and *actively choosing* to date someone with depressive tendencies. Unless you really know what you're letting yourself in for, dating a depressive is a long, hard road with few rewards. And this is why.

Depression is an incredibly frustrating disease. Unlike any other ailment, depression gets to the very heart of who you are. It skews your perspective of the world, making everything seem bleak, difficult or hopeless. But most of all, it makes you incredibly selfish. Your mind is constantly occupied with your own thoughts and doubts. Other people in your life become secondary to the depression because you feel so overwhelmed by its power. There's no cheering up to be done. There's no pulling yourself together.

Some women are drawn to depressives because they seem so dark and mysterious. Women want to mother them, take care of them, cheer them up. Perhaps I can reach him? Maybe all he needs is a good listener? Maybe I'll be the one to make him happy when all other women have failed? Perhaps you will. But it's a huge risk and are you sure you want to take it?

My experience of living with a depressive was heartbreaking. I loved him desperately and yet, in the end, his depression became bigger than I could cope with. He would spend hours preoccupied with the idea that the relationship was doomed. I, in turn, would spend hours cheerleading, rallying, convincing him that things would get better. On bad days he was hugely oversensitive – I'd have to walk on conversational eggshells or face interrogation about "What did I mean when I said … ?" The mood swings were exhausting. The endless talking through of things, going round in conversational circles, the self-defeating statements and gloomy predictions. He would spend long periods of time by himself, cutting me off, keeping out of contact. I felt myself being sucked into his depression; I began to feel hopeless and trapped too. All my optimism and confidence started to ebb away.

Depression is not something you can solve by yourself. Like heart disease or diabetes, it's a disease that needs professional help if it's going to get better. It's also a problem that you need to understand fully if you're going to tackle it – you need to learn as much as you can about the condition. It takes the patience of a saint and the heart of a lion to deal with a depressive. You need to be vigilant, tough, and ready to play a long game. I'm not saying you can't do it. But I am saying that you need to be absolutely *crystal clear* about what you're letting yourself in for. Personally, I never want to go there again.

" Although by no means my longest relationship, Jeremy was probably the most traumatic. When we met I had no idea he had any mental health problems nor that he was unhappy. He seemed a confident young man with a good job. We started seeing each other and it was great, although I always sensed he was keeping something back or he was projecting an image of what he wanted me to see.

We had an accident and I got pregnant. I'll never forget the day I told him, he responded with 'Well actually I have something to tell you. I have been to the doctors and he says I am depressed.' It was a strange reaction but I was worried about him so I dealt with the trauma of the abortion alone, whilst trying to support him and help him stay positive.

The next six months were a rollercoaster ride of him going missing for days or even weeks at a time; or being very angry and trying to start fights with people; drinking too much then not drinking anything. I was so stressed by it all and very angry. I made a decision to break the relationship off as it was clearly not working, although we did try to remain friends.

Four weeks after our relationship broke down, Jeremy committed suicide. There was no note and no explanation but it was certainly no cry for help. The way he did it made it clear it was planned. I know that I was not the reason for this, and I also know he was not a well person. But moving on has been so difficult; I worry about people all the time and believe the worst has happened if I do not hear back from someone immediately. The stress and trauma in being involved with someone with mental health problems were exhausting and the repercussions have lasted for years. There is also always the niggling question – what could I have done differently that might have saved him?""

Rachel

• MR SPONGER •

"Got any spare change love?" Hardly the words you want to hear from the future father of your children. And yet loads of us seem happy to date spongers, men who can't seem to rustle up enough for a latte never mind a lasting relationship.

Don't get me wrong. Money can't buy you love. And dating someone based on their bank balance is about as shallow as you can get. But there's a big difference between gold digging and expecting your partner to pull his financial weight.

Long gone are the days when men were expected to support women. And rightly so. Suffragettes didn't lash themselves to railings just so we could stay at home filing our nails. But are you really saying you're happy to take on the role of sole provider, when he won't even get out of bed?

Suffragettes didn't lash themselves to railings just so we could stay at home filing our nails.

In long-term relationships, partners rarely earn exactly the same. That's normal. In a committed set-up, you both sit down and work out how to best divide your time, skills and money. If kids or a career change come along, this discussion becomes even more important and it's not unusual for the higher-earning partner to carry on working while the lower-paid parent stays at home. Whether that's the man or the woman is neither here nor there. The point is that you're both pulling your weight and planning a future together.

Mr Sponger is not a stay-at-home-dad in the making. He's not taking a back seat to allow your career to progress. He's not even earning less to make you look good. He's simply allowing you to take care of him, the way a parent gives out pocket money.

But he's a struggling artist. His band is his life. He's not into material things. He's following his dream. Really? Isn't it funny how so many blokes who live on fresh air actually have generous girlfriends? He might have renounced capitalism but he doesn't seem to have a problem with you paying his bills. He can only indulge his interests whilst he's got someone to bankroll them. Do you really want to be handing over his beer money when you've got a mortgage, childcare and food to pay for too? Beware of signing up for a life of heavy responsibility with little support. Believe me, when you're 50 and still living in a manky bedsit together, the appeal of unusual sex and a bit of guitar playing will have long worn off. What is it that Mae West said? "Love conquers all things except poverty and toothache."

People who follow a creative dream or take a career break, *and make a success of it*, are those who are completely realistic about what it takes. It's damned hard work and you can't simply expect someone else to pick up the tab. Lots of people who follow their dream have to swallow their pride and take a second job or a huge pay cut. They plan. They budget. They work all the hours God sends. They live within their means. And they certainly don't expect their loved ones to fund their lifestyle. There's also nothing to be ashamed of if you find yourself suddenly broke – it can happen to all of us – but please don't make it a lifestyle choice.

66 I dated someone who fell into three of these categories: The Sponger. The Player. The Addict. A struggling jazz pianist, so naturally a Sponger. (His favourite joke was: 'What's a musician without a girlfriend? Broke!' Oh how we laughed.) A Player – definitely a tad too friendly with every waitress and barmaid in our area, who would view me with undisguised pity whenever we frequented their places of work. And an Addict – smoked and drank more than anyone I've ever seen. (He once met me off an aeroplane at Heathrow not with roses but two cans of Stella in his jacket pocket. The romance.) I fell for him like a ton of bricks within weeks – but I finally came to my senses a mere three months later and stopped texting him. But it took me about a year to get over him, which beats all date-to-break-up-recovery ratio laws. I still think about him from time to time, even though I'm happily paired up

with a wonderful, loving man now. If he rang me tomorrow, I honestly don't know what I'd do. "

Gina

• MR MUMMY'S BOY •

He's gorgeous. He's successful. He thinks you're the bee's knees. So why does he still keep getting phone calls from his mum checking whether he's wearing clean underpants?

It's lovely when your bloke gets on with his mother. I've been out with enough men who didn't like their parents to know what a relief it is when your man has a healthy, happy relationship with his family. But blokes who still take their washing home every Sunday, can't make a decision without consulting mum or, even worse, still live at home in their thirties are bad news.

Ahhh…but he loves his mummy. Great. But are you sure you're ready for a relationship where there are three of you involved? When he asks if you want to come back to his place, do you really want to spend a night of wild passion rolling around under a Spiderman duvet? Are you truly ready to watch your potential life partner undergo constant spit-washes and tie straightening?

Do you really want to spend a night of wild passion rolling around under a Spiderman duvet?

Face it. You'll never be the woman of his dreams. He's already got one. His mother raised him to be the centre of her world, her little prince to be indulged at every turn. This isn't mother love, it's smother love and she'll want to be involved in every aspect of his life whether you like it or not. If he attempts to break free or show independence, she'll use her best weapon – guilt. He'll be forced to take sides and, guess what, it won't be yours. You'll always be the other woman.

It's easy to see why a mother would find it difficult to let go of her son – she's spent her life protecting, nurturing and providing for him, and may find it hard to accept that her role has changed. If her husband or partner turned out to be a lifelong disappointment, it's no wonder she threw herself into raising her children.

But what drives Mr Mummy's Boy in return? Why is he struggling to cut those apron strings? Easy. He doesn't want to. Who wouldn't like someone waiting on them hand and foot? How lovely to have a permanent housekeeper catering to your every whim. There's been many a time when I'm stuffing soiled pants into my Hotpoint and I've thought it would be lovely to have full-time hired help (preferably butch and Swedish). But real life isn't like that.

You need a bloke who'll put you, not his mater, first. You want someone who isn't expecting to be mollycoddled or mothered. You want a partner who won't leave you with mountains of washing up, whilst still expecting you to work a full week. Stick with Mr Mummy's Boy and you'll spend the rest of your life picking up the pieces and his dirty Y-fronts.

" I dated a guy called Richard who, at 28, was still living with his mother. She'd separated from Richard's dad when the boys were still young and cast herself as a Peggy Mitchell character. Her boys were her life. She tolerated me but made it clear that I wasn't ever going to be good enough to marry her darling son. Richard was really protective of his mum and I think she took advantage of this – always asking for lifts everywhere, constantly texting him, etc. The final straw came when we were fooling around in his bedroom. She barged in without knocking, clutching a bunch of coat hangers, and proceeded to slowly hang them up in his wardrobe. The fact that I was naked and straddling him didn't seem to bother her, or Richard for that matter. It was then that it occurred to me that perhaps our relationship wasn't normal. "

Andrea

• MR DOORMAT •

"I'll have what you're having. I don't mind darling, *you* choose. I want whatever you want."

Arghhhhhhhh. Someone kill me now. Mr Doormat, bless him, has to be one of the most irritating men you can date. It's not that he's horrible. He's probably a really nice guy. But spend long enough in his company and in no time you'll want to grab him by his shirt collar, shake him and scream, "For God's sake, grow a pair!"

Mr Doormat, bless him, has to be one of the most irritating men you can date.

Being accommodating is an important life skill but it's not the same as being a pushover. The problem with Mr Doormat is that he's turned people-pleasing into a fine art, often at the expense of his own happiness. Do you really want to date someone who invests so much in outside approval that he's lost all sense of his own wants and needs? How will he ever reach his own personal goals when he's too busy saying yes to everyone else's?

Just being a nice person doesn't explain the self-sabotaging element of being such a softy, so what *really* motivates Mr Doormat? People who make a career out of pleasing others are often looking for validation, they can't judge the value of their own actions so they need someone else to do it for them. The roots of this are often laid down in childhood – kids who aren't encouraged to think for themselves or assert their own needs, and are rewarded for consistently obeying the rules, learn that compliance is the quickest way to people's hearts. Don't rock the boat. Don't tell people how you really feel. Defer to everyone else's judgement. These are the tools a people-pleaser uses to gain social acceptance and love.

So what are the classic signs that you're dating Mr Doormat? Does he hide his feelings so as not to upset you? Does he leave it up to you to initiate intimacy? Does he avoid arguments at all costs? Does he go blank when you ask him what he thinks, likes or wants? Does he go into himself when he's annoyed? Does he constantly bombard people with compliments? Or find it difficult to turn down a request, however inconvenient? Does he do all this but then moan to you about how much he's taken on or how many people take him for granted? If so, it's looks like you've gone and netted yourself a wet fish.

So what's the problem? Is it really so bad to date someone who always puts your needs ahead of theirs? Well, there are two nasty surprises that come with dating Mr Doormat. The first is that you're essentially dating a liar. They're simply not being honest with you about their own feelings and needs. How can you have a relationship with someone who feels they can't tell you the truth? It's Mr Liar Liar rearing his ugly head again.

The second sticking point comes when Mr Doormat finally has enough of people-pleasing and bites back. Being endlessly accommodating will eventually take its toll and there's a good chance he'll boil over at some stage. When a doormat explodes, it's often a total surprise for the other person – it's the old cliché of the passive-aggressive Stepford wife finally snapping or the timid husband turning into a tyrant. They never see it coming and neither will you.

66 My experience of dating a doormat was brief but left a lasting impression. We met at uni, he was a guy in our circle of friends. Everyone knew that he had a crush on me and part of me was just thrilled to have the attention.

It's interesting but he expressed his own opinions with other people but then agreed with absolutely everything I said. It was quite flattering at first but it didn't take long before it got really annoying. Any view I had, he'd agree with. My interests were suddenly *his* interests. It's actually very difficult to have a conversation with someone who doesn't bounce ideas back or offer a different point of view.

I hate to say it, but his doormat tendencies brought out a really horrible side in me. On only the second date I was already looking for an argument just to spark some kind of response from him. My attempts were futile and in sheer desperation I snapped and yelled 'You don't have a f**king opinion about anything do you?' And guess what? He agreed. "

Naomi

• MR CHILD HATER •

Is it just me or are men who *hate* kids just a little bit weird? It's like hating puppies or baby chicks – Walt Disney made cartoon villains out of nicer characters. It's one thing for him not to want kids or to prefer the company of adults, but do you really want to date *Chitty Chitty Bang Bang*'s child catcher?

Kids can be noisy, smelly, obnoxious and irritating. But they're still kids. It's not like they're man-eating tigers. What's going on in a bloke's head that would make him so vehemently anti-children? Be indifferent by all means, but *hate*? That's a strong emotion and I'm not sure I like what it means for a relationship.

Even if your bloke doesn't ever want to have a family, saying that you hate any group of people is a sweeping statement, usually based on ignorance. If he said the same thing about an ethnic group, he'd be strung up by his short and curlies, and rightly so. Do you really want to date someone who writes off an entire section of society without thinking?

Hating kids is also peculiar because children are such a vulnerable group – it's like hating the elderly. Why doesn't he pick on someone his own size? Even if you don't end up having children as a couple, it's difficult to avoid contact with kids for the rest of your lives together. What's he going to do when nephews, nieces or friends' children come round to visit – lock himself in the bathroom?

And what if you end up having children together? If your partner won't co-parent, you're in big trouble – there's no way he'll be able to love, nurture and tolerate your kids to the extent he needs to. He won't put in the investment your children will demand, leaving everyone in the family feeling short-changed. At worst, he might even be hostile or violent – an unforgivable environment in which to raise kids.

Don't confuse Mr Child Hater with a bloke who has simply decided that being a father isn't for him. If you are both clear from the beginning that that's what you want, great. It takes a lot of courage to make such a bold life choice and you should respect the decision he's made. If your current squeeze is adamant about not wanting children, however, and you are pretty sure you do at some stage, then you may have to face the fact that this relationship probably isn't going anywhere. Getting pregnant in the hope that he'll change his mind in the delivery suite is a gamble no-one in their right mind would take.

> 66 Philip, my ex, constantly talked about other people's kids as 'little shits' or 'rugrats'. At first I thought he was joking but I soon realised he was being serious. He absolutely loathed being around children – he didn't know how to relate to them so I think he found it easier to be horrible than make an effort. He also used to hate hearing kids being noisy, even

if they were just messing about and enjoying themselves. Things started to unravel when he talked with great affection about how his dad used to whack him with a bicycle inner tube as punishment and that, if he had any kids, he'd have no hesitation doing the same. All the time I was thinking 'Not with any of my kids you won't.' It makes me feel sick if I think about whether Phil went on to have children with anyone else. "

Celia

• MR ADDICT •

I must get myself an addiction. It seems anyone who's anyone has one. I was thinking of becoming addicted to brie … it seems as if anything goes. Addiction to shopping. Addiction to internet porn. I even read of someone addicted to tanning salons.

But I'm not entirely convinced these are addictions. Habits possibly. Excuses definitely. I suspect that calling them addictions helps 'victims' feel it's not their fault. If they convince themselves that their behaviour is out of their hands, they're no longer culpable. We've become a nation of excuse-makers.

So what do we mean when we talk about real addiction? Forget the odd blow-out in Harvey Nics, a true addiction is a physical or psychological dependence on a substance or behaviour. The dependence is so crippling you can't stop it, even if it's killing your body, livelihood or relationships. If left untreated, addiction will destroy everything it touches – home life, children, career, health. It almost seems pointless to spell out the reasons why dating Mr Addict is bad news but humour me.

People become addicts for a whole host of reasons. The nature of addiction isn't fully understood but it seems as if lots of different factors come into play. A genetic predisposition is one possibility – the idea that you might have an inherently addictive personality. Childhood and poor parenting matter too – the children of alcoholics, for example, are four times more likely to become addicted to drink. Peer pressure, low self-esteem, stress, emotional turmoil – these are all reasons why people turn to addiction.

Certain substances, such as nicotine or heroin, also cause chemical changes in the brain, creating cravings that are very difficult to overcome. You might only intend to try drugs once or twice but the very nature of a substance can make it impossible to simply take it or leave it.

Spotting an addict isn't always as easy as you might think. Not all drug addicts end up in the gutter. Lots of drunks hold down high-powered jobs; of all the professions – from brickies to bus drivers – it's actually lawyers who are most likely to turn alcoholic. With so much at stake, you need to be alert to the signs that suggest a potential partner might have a problem.

Sooner or later, however, the non-stop party turns into non-stop hell.

When you first meet him, Mr Addict might seem like the life and soul of the party. He's everybody's friend, always the first on the invite list and the last to go to bed. You don't know how he keeps going. Sooner or later, however, the non-stop party turns into non-stop hell.

Sometimes the clues might be physical – depending on the addiction, your bloke might begin to rapidly lose or gain weight, take less care of his appearance, or start to look less healthy. The changes can be psychological too – becoming more irritable, secretive, angry or detached. Addiction has a way of isolating sufferers from the people around them – you may notice him becoming distant or moody, especially if he's being kept away from the object of his addiction.

Addiction is a nightmare. I wouldn't wish it on anyone. But dating an addict is equally grim. Mr Addict is self-centred to the extreme. His obsession – whether it's downing booze or looking at boobs – is more important than anything else. The addiction will never allow you to come first.

Mr Addict can't even connect with himself emotionally, let alone anyone else. He's got no self-control and no limits. He'll try to cover his tracks or evade responsibility, when all the time he's destroying himself and taking you with him. Date an addict and you'll always be at the mercy of their rollercoaster existence – some days are great, some days are horrendous. Life with an addict is like a box of poisoned chocolates – you never know what you're gonna get.

> 66 I was still at school when I met Tom. He was 21. I didn't fancy him at first but did think he was really cool because he had an amazing car, lived by himself and was always having wild parties. I also really loved his family – my dad was drinking really heavily at that time so it was difficult to be at home. Ironically, despite the fact that Tom was a safe haven in one sense, he was also a heavy drinker too. He'd come home from work on a Friday night and go straight out to the local

pub and get absolutely shit-faced. I can remember he'd often wet himself in bed – he even lost his licence because of drink-driving.

When I started to quiz him about it, he always turned it around to me, saying that I was over-sensitive about drink because of my dad. He often covered his own faults by drawing attention to mine or by picking at little things. Apparently I was 'no fun'. All of Tom's family were big drinkers – their get-togethers at home revolved around alcohol – so he didn't think he had a problem. Drink also made him incredibly selfish – I was spending an increasing amount of time on my own while he was down at the pub. By the last two years of the relationship I wasn't really part of his life, so there wasn't much point sticking around. I think I'd also grown-up a lot from that 14-year-old girl and could see that there was more to life than sitting around waiting for a drunk to stagger home."

Abigail

• MR NEVER BEEN SINGLE •

You've met a wonderful bloke. He's never been unfaithful to a girlfriend. He loves being in love. He's proud to declare himself a 'one-woman man'. The only problem is that it's been one woman after another after another.

Mr Never Been Single takes serial monogamy to a whole new level. From the moment his testicles started their journey south, he's barely spent a moment to himself. He's been chain-smoking girlfriends – from the embers of one dying relationship he sparks the beginnings of another. Ask how long he's spent being a bachelor and he'll struggle to give you an answer. He's so happy being part of a couple it would never occur to him that he needed to spend time on his own.

> ## From the moment his testicles started their journey south, he's barely spent a moment to himself.

But why does it matter whether a bloke has invested enough time in being single? Surely dating Mr Never Been Single is better than shacking up with someone who's completely new to the game? Well, yes and no.

There's no doubt that a serial monogamist feels comfy in coupledom. But is he really interested in any meaningful, long-term commitment? For him, the best bit about a relationship is the first flush of romance. Nothing equals the thrill of meeting a new person, falling head over heels and bonking each other senseless. But what happens when the honeymoon period wears off? How can the reality of long-term commitment ever compete with the novelty of a new fling? What does it say about someone if they can repeatedly love you one minute and leave you the next?

I once heard serial monogamy being compared to hiring a car instead of buying one – the problem is that if you know you're not going to keep it forever, you don't treat it very well. Mr Never Been Single is using serial monogamy as a way of getting regular, hassle-free sex without any of the inconveniences of long-term commitment. Romantic, eh?

Even those serial monogamists who stay in relationships for significant lengths of time have a problem with the concept of 'forever'. They like the sense of security that comes with being part of a couple but don't want to make any long-term plans. You might even be living together but don't expect wedding bells any time soon. His commitment is essentially superficial. Do you really want to be dating someone with such blatant attachment issues?

The second problem with Mr Never Been Single is that he hasn't spent enough time on his own. Being single is a hugely important time for reflection and personal development (we'll look at this in more detail in Chapter 4). We also need time to learn lessons from a relationship when it ends. This isn't going to happen if the bloke immediately throws himself into the arms of another woman. Is the fear of being lonely keeping him in an endless cycle of relationships? Does he only have an identity when he's part of a couple? It's not going to do your self-esteem any good if you suspect he's only using you as his plus-one.

Believe it or not, Mr Never Been Single and Mr Player have a lot in common. The only difference tends to be how many women they've got on the go at any one time. While a serial monogamist will at least do you the honour of keeping his trousers on when you're not there, he's still an STD waiting to happen. As US sexpert Yvonne Fulbright helpfully noted:

> "I have friends who are serial monogamists and in every monogamous relationship, sex eventually becomes unprotected ... Sooner or later, having put themselves at risk for STDs or HIV, they break up and move on to the next partner where the same thing happens."

So how do you spot Mr Never Been Single? A quick browse through his dating résumé should ring alarm bells. Has he spent any periods of time being single? What was his longest relationship? If both of these can only be measured in weeks or months, walk on by. Don't expect him, however, to be shy and retiring. Most serial monogamists tend to be outgoing, social and impulsive – how else do you think they meet so many women? They're also often drawn to high-octane activities and new challenges – whether it's sports, work or women. Face it, dating this guy is going to be the equivalent of a white water rafting experience – bumpy, exciting, and over just as you were beginning to enjoy yourself.

" I met David when I first moved to London. I was lonely and finding it hard to meet new friends. Suddenly there was this wonderful man who thought I was wonderful too. For six months he swooped me off my feet, proudly introduced me to his friends, asked me round to his place nearly every night, cooked wonderful meals. He did incredible things like taking me off for romantic weekends or simply endlessly stroking my hair and telling me how amazing I was, and asking what on earth he did before I was in his life. I even got to meet the parents and stayed with them for a weekend – they were lovely and made me feel so welcome.

I had singed fingers from previous relationships and was keeping my cards close to my chest as to how I felt about him, but as time went by more and more of my fears were allayed and I started to trust that this paragon was 'the real thing'. FINALLY! HOORAY.

So at around month six, as we were snuggled up together on a Sunday morning, I looked into his eyes and stroked back the adorable lock of black hair that fell over his forehead and said 'Gosh I really do like you.'

The panic in his eyes was almost funny. He couldn't get out of the place quickly enough and suddenly had something pressing to do that day. By the following Wednesday I was dumped, fairly unceremoniously, because I was taking things too fast. ARRRRRRRGGGGG!"

Charlotte

• YOU'VE BEEN WARNED •

Most of this book is about unravelling the reasons behind bad dating and changing those destructive patterns. You can rarely force people to change, and nor should you, but you can alter how *you* deal with situations and emotions. That said, it's also helpful to be given a head start in terms of the type of men you should avoid if you want a truly happy ending. You can totally alter the way you approach dating *but* if you keep choosing these types of frogs, you're asking for trouble. Don't say you haven't been warned.

• • •

2

Chapter Two

ONCE UPON A TIME . . .

. . .

So, now you know that frogs come in all shapes and sizes. It's time to dig deep and have a look at how little princesses learn about relationships.

There's no point trying to make any progress finding Mr Right if we keep making the same mistakes over and over again. Poking about in your past can be about as comfortable as a bikini wax but don't freak out – all we're doing here is trying to understand why we keep falling into the same trap. Why do we behave the way we do in relationships? If we've got bad habits, where are they coming from?

> **Poking about in your past can be about as comfortable as a bikini wax.**

• HOW LITTLE PRINCESSES LEARN • ABOUT LOVE

We learn about love from a huge variety of sources. In fact, we never stop learning. Some life experiences will be more profound than others, and it can be very difficult to unravel where your attitudes come from. Were you influenced by fairy stories or teen magazines when you were growing up, for example? Have previous relationships affected how you behave in present romances?

We're complex creatures and the reality is that *who* you are now is a mishmash of lots of different experiences. While you'll probably never identify every single influence, let's look at some factors that might ring some bells. It's food for thought if nothing else.

Perhaps the best place to start is to look at how our families have influenced our ideas about what an adult relationship should look and feel like. From the moment of our birth, we start to build up a picture of what it means to be a man or a woman and how the different sexes should relate to each other. Children absorb and interpret the adult relationships that surround them and, for most kids, mums and dads are the primary role models. Taking a sneaky peek at how your parents related to each other might just give you a few clues as to why you're in a pickle now.

• SO MUCH OF WHAT WE KNOW • OF LOVE WE LEARN AT HOME

The misanthropic poet, Philip Larkin, wrote:

"They f**k you up, your mum and dad.
They may not mean to, but they do.
They fill you with the faults they had.
And add some extra, just for you."

Christ, that's depressing. Larkin was a miserable bugger and few of us are unlucky enough to feel the way he did about his upbringing. And yet many of us still have mixed-up views about what it means to love another person. I know I do. So where have they come from?

Well, the reality is that *all* types of parenting have an effect of how children view relationships. Take the way that parents show affection, for example. Most parents feel very squishy about their kids, although some don't always know how to demonstrate it. Some parents opt for the school-of-hard-knocks approach, which assumes that kids need to be toughened up for whatever life throws at them. The assumption is that 'spoiling' children with too much emotional and physical affection, or failing to discipline them harshly, will leave them unable to cope in the real world – the old 'spare the rod, spoil the child' bollocks.

Other parents over-indulge their kids to compensate for what they regard as their own failings. We've all seen the cliché of the guilt-ridden parent who thinks mountains of gifts make up for months of absence. Anyone with half a brain knows that kids need your presence not your presents. Neither of these parenting extremes prepares us emotionally for the real world and can leave us with skewed ideas about how best to demonstrate that we care for someone. I like sparkly prezzies as much as the next magpie, but not if they come with emotional strings attached.

Parents can also give us very mixed messages about our lovableness. Perhaps you felt that you were only loveable if you got straight A's or looked pretty in pink? Maybe they conveyed the notion that their love was conditional on your being a 'good girl' or toeing the family line? Sometimes the messages are very subtle. Children often, for example, pick up on the idea that parents find it easy to love a child who reminds them of themselves. Perhaps your parents went the opposite way and showered you with praise even when you were behaving like a brat?

• THE RELATIONSHIP TOOLBOX •

Of course, our parents also influence our 'Emotional Intelligence' – how adept we are at understanding and dealing with our own emotions and those of others. Emotions such as empathy, sympathy, sensitivity to others, diplomacy and timing are all vital to successful relationships (and indeed other essential parts of life such as holding down a job, running a household or ordering a spritzer). These interpersonal skills are ones that, hopefully, we pick up from our family. We need someone to pass on these emotional 'tools' – otherwise we'll struggle to build sturdy relationships in the future.

If our parents are protective, supportive, loving, responsive and encouraging, it gives us the ammunition and self-esteem to go on to forge equally healthy relationships in later life. We learn how to speak in a loving way, show affection, ask for what we need, and how to give ourselves to others, without compromising our own happiness.

• THE CIRCLE OF STRIFE •

How your parents behaved with *each other* also has a crucial effect on your romantic dealings later in life. It doesn't necessarily follow that if your parents had a bad marriage, then you will too, but it can be difficult to break from the unhealthy lessons that are passed on. It's no surprise that children of divorced parents are more likely to get divorced themselves – if all you've experienced is parents constantly at war, that's what you're most likely to copy.

But let's not be too hard on divorcees, thank you very much (speaking as one myself). A healthy divorce can have a much more positive effect on children than parents staying together and being unhappy – after all, 18 years is a long time to spend in a family home with two parents who can't stand the sight of each other. The key point is that parents who bicker on a regular basis are setting their children up for potential problems in the future. Kids who are brought up in homes filled with parental conflict are more likely to go on to develop mental health problems, anger or anxiety. They tend to find it more difficult to have fulfilling, adult relationships in later life. Children in these families also often develop unhealthy coping strategies such as bottling up negative feelings or self-harming. (In Chapter 6 we learn some techniques for arguing constructively.)

But – and it is a BIG but – saying that your attitude to romance is a direct result of your childhood is too simplistic. For one thing, it doesn't take into account *your* personality and all the other factors that have influenced who you are today. The point is to think about how your parents related to each other and ask whether that has had any bearing on the type of men you are choosing today?

It can be a bit creepy making comparisons between boyfriends and your immediate family. But it's actually very helpful. Lots of us go for blokes who remind us of male relatives. It's the pull of the familiar. If I had a pound for every time a girlfriend said they wished they could meet someone like their father/brother, well, I'd have at least enough to buy a cup of tea and a cream horn. Anyway that's not the point. The reality is that we often go for men who remind us of our childhood and it's nothing to be ashamed of. If, however, you insist that every new boyfriend has to grow a fatherly beard, take up pipe smoking and become adept at marrow growing, I'm afraid you're going to need more help than I can offer.

The point is this. You need to ask yourself some searching questions. Am I looking for someone just like my father or am I looking for the complete opposite? Am I expecting to be treated in the same way that my parents treated each other – good or bad? Am I hoping that my Prince Charming will put me on a pedestal, like my family did, or am I realistic about my bad points? What roles were assigned to men and women in our household? Were girls and boys viewed equally?

• EMOTIONAL PORRIDGE •

Parenting isn't a sausage factory – no two kids are alike, even if you attempt to treat them the same way. But it's common sense that certain types of parenting will have broadly predictable results. Most parents fall into one of four very general categories, based on how well they balance the need to control their kids and how well they respond to what their children ask for.

> Parenting isn't a sausage factory – no two kids are alike, even if you attempt to treat them the same way.

To borrow a term coined by relationship guru Julia Cole, these different styles of parenting create different 'emotional porridge'. Just like the Goldilocks and the Three Bears story, some families are too hot, some families are too cold, and some families are just right. There are also some families who would sadly fit into 'the empty bowl' category. You'll see what I mean in a minute.

TOO COLD

Have you ever met a family where the parents are scarily strict? The authoritarian parents rule the roost in this house and the children are expected to do as they're told. Rules are harsh, inflexible, often inconsistent and rarely broken. Parents in these families tend to be unresponsive to the wishes of their children and see no reason to negotiate. They often use the tools of emotional punishment – guilt, shame, embarrassment – or physical punishment when a child crosses a boundary. And they also invariably find it difficult to show affection or enthusiasm for a child's achievements and yet they have high expectations of success.

How this might affect your choice of men: *From the outside you probably look like a high achiever. But under the surface, do you lack self-confidence and find social situations difficult, even if you've learned to hide it well? There's a good chance you push yourself academically or in your working life, but you may also struggle with self-esteem and be prone to depression. As an adolescent, did you rebel by leaving home or getting involved in risky behaviour such as drugs, truancy, crime or promiscuity? As an adult, are you attracted to men you know your parents would disapprove of or who make little demands on your time or affections? Or do you find it difficult to escape from the family mould and instead choose partners who are emotionally cool, controlling or dominating?*

TOO HOT

These are the kinds of families you never want to sit next to in a restaurant. The kids run amok while the parents watch on indulgently. They set very few boundaries for their children and yet are highly responsive to their little darlings' every whim. The parents demand very little in terms of good behaviour and show love by saying 'yes' to every request, however outrageous. Kids from permissive families have few limits on their behaviour and are therefore rarely punished. There's no shortage of affection in these households but the mums and dads tend to befriend their kids rather than parent them, feeling reluctant to enforce any kind of rules that would make them unpopular.

How this might affect your choice of men: *If you were raised in an indulgent home, you'll have no self-esteem problems and feel confident in social situations. Great. Unfortunately, because you have never been taught to control your own impulses, you often find it difficult to regulate your emotions or take responsibility for your behaviour in a grown-up relationship. Preferring the role of child to adult, you may choose father figures who cater to your every whim or opt for men who are easily dominated and forgive your indiscretions and outbursts. Partners may have accused you of being self-centred or immature, and you may be struggling to make the personal sacrifices needed for a happy, balanced long-term relationship.*

YUM – JUST RIGHT

In these families there are clear rules and you know where the line is, but the parents are prepared to compromise and adapt to the changing needs of a growing child. As well as rules, these parents teach their child about decision-making and self-sufficiency. Trust, communication and respect are encouraged on both sides, and parents in these families tend to use positive parenting – such as rewarding good behaviour – instead of harsh punishments. Families in these scenarios also tend to find it easy to show warmth and encouragement, accepting mistakes as part of the learning process.

How this might affect your choice of men: *You are one of the lucky ones. If you grew up in a family like this, you'll be a good communicator, content, and well balanced. You'll tend to do well in relationships with others because you are happy with yourself and find it easy to demonstrate love. You find it easy to empathise – making you a good candidate for a long-term relationship – and you tend to choose men who make you feel good about yourself rather than fill any self-destructive need. You tend to be emotionally resilient, making it possible to recover from failed relationships and you'll feel able to try again. If you've struggled to make a long-term relationship last, perhaps there are other issues holding you back, some of which we'll look at next.*

AN EMPTY BOWL

At their very worst, these types of parents are either neglectful or abusive. They are both undemanding and unresponsive – they expect nothing from their children and give nothing in return. An uninvolved parent may provide all the basics of life – food and shelter – but remain emotionally uninterested in their child's life.

How this might affect your choice of men: *If this sounds familiar, you're a ruddy hero, just for surviving your childhood with your sanity intact. People with uninvolved parents tend to struggle in most areas of life, including love and family life, and may find themselves repeating the toxic cycle of abusive or uncaring relationships. Quite understandably, you may find it difficult to trust others or attach yourself to someone romantically, perhaps finding it hard to control aggressive tendencies or self-destructive behaviour. The good news, however, is that you're a natural survivor and by simply picking up this book you've* *demonstrated that you're not hell-bent on repeating your parents' mistakes. Perhaps it's time to take things even further and talk to a trained counsellor about how to put your past behind you?*

The reality of family life is that your parents may not fit neatly into any of these categories – perhaps they've demonstrated different styles of parenting at different times. Even the best parents can go through phases of being uninvolved, for example, if work is really stressful or money worries take over. Brothers and sisters, or stepchildren and biological children, in the same family can also receive different styles of parenting under the same roof – it's almost impossible to treat siblings in exactly the same way even if you try. All families are different but the idea of 'emotional porridge' might explain, at least in part, where some of your ideas and patterns about blokes come from.

• PUPPY LOVE •

Parents are often an easy target when it comes to blame. But as I said at the start of this chapter, there's a huge range of other life experiences that affect how we behave in adult relationships.

When things are going wrong in a current relationship, do you find yourself fantasising about a first love? Do you still compare all new partners to that first teenage boyfriend? Perhaps in moments of loneliness, you even think about getting in touch or trying to find their name on Facebook?

If any of this sounds familiar, you're in good company. Over half of us regularly fantasise about our first love. First loves are truly, madly, deeply thrilling. They also move us to write some really *really* bad poetry. But why do they hold such sway when we can barely remember what they looked like?

• THE FIRST CUT IS THE DEEPEST •

The legacy of your first love is lasting for a number of reasons. For one thing, your first real relationship tends to coincide with your adolescence – a period of rampant hormones, sprouting hair and self-discovery. Your first boyfriend is usually the first person you attach yourself to outside of the immediate family; so how they treat you can have a huge effect on how you feel about yourself. They become part of your identity and when the relationship ends – at is does in 99 per cent of cases – it can feel like a rejection of your entire self.

When teenagers fall in love, the experience mimics the strong bond between mother and infant. First loves are overwhelming, exciting and unusually intense. It's impossible to recreate that first flush of romance in later life, although many of us spend fruitless hours trying. Some scientists have even compared teens in love to taking cocaine. Pathways light up in the brain when we first experience romantic feelings which have a similar effect as using coke. It seems love *really* is a drug.

The outcome of these first loves can have a huge impact on the rest of our adult lives, affecting how we love and who. They can even set the standard by which we measure future partners or establish patterns we follow time and time again.

• DUMPED UNCEREMONIOUSLY •

Puppy love certainly had a profound effect on me. My first boyfriend and I went out for two years between the ages of

14 and 16. It sounds like schoolgirl stuff now, but when he snogged someone else and dropped me like a stone I was absolutely devastated. Two years is a long time in the life of a teenager and I couldn't imagine how I'd go back to being single again – so much of my identity was wrapped up in being part of a couple. Before we'd got together I'd been invisible at school. All it took was a bad perm, trowels of make-up and a fit bloke on my arm and everything had changed for the better.

It sounds utterly ridiculous but I've never been as disorientated by a break-up since, even when my ex-husband and I decided to go our separate ways. At 16, I felt totally rejected and from then on expected all relationships to end the same way. Whether I subconsciously chose young men who weren't fully committed or behaved in ways that reinforced my own feelings of inadequacy, I don't know, but the end result was that for the next 15 years I dated, loved and married men who didn't really love me as much as I loved them.

Rejection came as no surprise – it only served to confirm what I already thought about myself, that I was easy to fall out of love with. Even now, when I'm happily married to a wonderful man, in my darkest moments I still get the fear that one day he'll leave too. You've got to admit those are pretty strong repercussions for what was essentially a daft teenage romance between two very young people.

• BEGINNER'S LUCK •

Other people have sickeningly blissful experiences of first love. In fact, their first relationships are so unrealistic that it can be difficult to reconcile the realities of adult life.

Grown-up relationships can be difficult, hard work and messy – we often yearn for that first love when we feel dissatisfied or frustrated with our current lot. Your first love is immortalised as the perfect partner, and precious years can be wasted hankering after a fantasy that doesn't exist. Few people who meet up with their first loves again find that the relationship can live up to expectations. We're simply not the same people we were as teenagers. For a start, my arse is about twice the size it was.

> Few people who meet up with their first loves again find that the relationship can live up to expectations.

So what can you do to protect yourself from the legacy of first love? Bar skipping your first relationship and waking up in your second, the best thing to do is to be super-realistic about why the idea of your first love seems so appealing. If you find yourself harking back to a first love, you need to ask yourself 'Why?' Are you dissatisfied with a current relationship? Do you find the reality of adult relationships too difficult? Are you choosing men who remind you of him, even if you're not the same person anymore? Resolving these issues might help you make better choices next time.

• FRIENDS AND FRENEMIES •

People outside your family and first loves also have a far-reaching effect on your choice of men. As teenagers, our friends become as important as family and we develop our own ways of talking, dressing and behaving, helping us to feel part of an exclusive club. Peer pressure can even exert an influence over our choice of boyfriends at that age. You might have felt obliged to only date guys who were viewed as good looking, 'dangerous' or popular, even though you really preferred the geek with the glasses. It's difficult enough to march to the beat of your own drum when you're an adult but it's almost impossible when you're facing social death at school.

And as we grow up, we still take our friends' views to heart. Few of us call our parents when relationships are rocky; instead we're straight on the blower to our best mates, happy to spend hours analysing the minutiae of what went wrong. There's only one thing worse than introducing a new man to your gang of girlfriends: that's introducing a new man to your girlfriends and them hating him. The idea of 'It's Me & Him Against the World' might feel deliciously romantic to start with, but isolating yourself from chums is rarely a recipe for long-term happiness. It's important to us that our boyfriends and husbands are given our girlfriends' seal of approval.

If we're lucky, friends have our best interests at heart – they can spot a frog at twenty paces and are happy to tell you when you've bagged one. Good friends often know you better than you know yourself and it can be refreshing to get the cold hard truth when your handsome prince is just a well-dressed frog in disguise.

But friendship is a double-edged sword, or it can be. Some friends can have their own agendas when it comes to imparting relationship advice. Perhaps they feel threatened that if you are loved up, they'll lose your friendship. Perhaps a friend has designs on your date? Perhaps they're scared your friendship will change for the worse if you find emotional intimacy elsewhere? Friends with a toxic edge aren't real friendships – they're frenemies – but they can have a strong influence on who we date, how long the relationship lasts, and how we feel about ourselves.

It can cut the other way too – perhaps your friends prefer you to be in a relationship? Double-dating is a hoot and it can really throw a spanner in the works if you stop being part of a couple. No-one likes a gooseberry tagging along.

Even if a friend's motives aren't as cynical or explicit as these, it can be difficult to make clear decisions about a potential relationship when you've got 'advice' flying in from all directions. Comments such as 'He's not really *you* is he?' aren't necessarily helpful if you're trying to break old dating habits and explore different kinds of relationships. It can also be tricky to try a new dating strategy if it breaches the religious, class or ethnic boundaries of your peer group.

Friendships are an essential part of who we are. They offer us intimacy, support and acceptance. They're also a huge source of fun. But just remember that, at the end of the day, however much your pals love or loath your bloke, there can only ever be two of you in the relationship. You need to plot your own course.

• BIG BANGS •

Feeling good about yourself is a huge part of being in a successful relationship. The higher your self-esteem, the better placed you are to make good decisions about relationships.

When you feel good about yourself, you tend to choose men who support this positive view.

Sadly, though, life has a nasty habit of throwing the most unwelcome surprises at you. I call these 'big bangs' – those experiences so profound that they can devastate your world and continue to have an influence months or even years after the event. Bereavement, divorce, serious illness, accidents and redundancy can all pull the rug from under you and give your self-esteem a real pounding.

A healthy amount of self-confidence can help us ride out most of life's ups and downs. But when these big bangs hit, they get stored in our brain in a particularly persistent way. The result is that they can have a huge effect on our behaviour and can place serious restrictions on the way we go about our lives. This, in turn, may affect the romantic choices we make.

To avoid feeling hurt again, we often avoid making ourselves emotionally vulnerable. This includes falling in love. After an emotional disaster, some of us go through periods of choosing undemanding relationships or men who don't attempt to scratch under the surface of who we are. We may avoid relationships altogether or simply hop between one-night stands to avoid any kind of real intimacy.

The bad news is that these negative memories can never truly be erased. (Although scientists are working on a pill which does just that … *seriously*.) The good news, though, is that you can lessen their impact by actively replacing them with positive memories. Surrounding yourself with good friends, fulfilling work, passions and pleasures will slowly lessen the effects of an unhappy trauma. In other words, you can move bad memories to the bottom drawer of your brain's filing cabinet, making them less likely to be at the forefront of your mind. It's also heartening to know that life events, even horrible ones, make us much more interesting, complex people. We learn from our mistakes and our memories. I'd much rather know someone with a few battle scars than someone who's never had to fight back from the pain of loss, fear or disappointment.

• FAIRY STORIES •

Besides family and friendships, what are our role models for relationships? Books? Cinema? TV? Magazines? As a nation we thrive on a peculiar mixture of kiss-and-tell exposés and sugary chick-flicks. Neither is a true reflection of relationships and yet many of us find it difficult not to be drawn into the illusion.

Influences come in many forms. Religion, media, education, literature and so on. Every element of our culture has the opportunity to teach us something about love and relationships and yet there seem to be fewer positive messages than at any time. If you spent a week analysing the content of every media story about relationships, for example, what would be the overwhelming messages? Boobs always win over brains. Screw someone for everything they've got. Knob size is everything. And violent relationships with celebs pay if the price is right. Doesn't exactly warm the cockles does it?

In the past, religion offered a strong moral framework about relationships and marriage. Even if you struggle with the Church's central message (as Homer Simpson said "Why should I spend half my Sunday hearing about how I'm going to Hell?"), you can't deny that some of the most deliciously heartwarming ideas about love have their basis in its teachings. I certainly don't want to get into a debate about the pros and cons of secularisation but it's interesting to think about what's filling the void that religion is leaving.

Who teaches us about relationships and love now? Sex education is thankfully high on the agenda in most schools but tends to say little about what it means *emotionally* to be in an adult relationship. Most 10-year-olds can slip a condom on a banana but very few will get any valuable advice about dating, love and commitment. The government also tends to steer well clear of any kind of moral guidance – it's a political hot potato and, as a nation, we're deeply suspicious of being told how to behave.

So it's left up to literature and the media to open our eyes. Unfortunately, real relationships rarely make good TV or a thrilling read. We get hugely mixed messages from what we watch and digest. Writer and comedian Sharon Hogan puts it brilliantly:

> "Romantic comedies are good-looking, they're pretty, but essentially they're just lying, and that's why we like them. Sometimes you can escape into them for a few hours and pretend that life's really like that. Except it's not. Because nobody sees the romcom couple 10 years down the line, when they've stopped having sex because one of them is angry that their career never took off and the other has porked out."

In seems that good relationships make rubbish TV. Screenwriter Lisa Holdsworth explains:

"Love and romance motivate the majority of the storylines in most dramas and films. But writers aren't interested in getting couples together. We want to keep them apart as long as possible. That's why TV romances are full of heartbreaking misunderstandings and devastating obstacles.

The writers have kept us all tuning in week after week (series after series in some cases) hoping that this will be the episode where they finally get it on! But the truth is, once they've said 'I love you' and shared a kiss, we writers lose interest. Or we split them up and go through it all again until we decide to get them back together.

Actually, what we writers are doing is providing a terrible template for real-life relationships. Those ridiculous misunderstandings designed to keep the couple apart? They could be solved with some proper communication. Those overwhelming obstacles? They could be warning signs that this couple shouldn't even be together. But the worst thing we do is suggest that once the couple are together, everything will be hunky-dory and we needn't watch them anymore. When we all know that is when the real work starts."

Romantic fiction fares little better. While few modern women can swallow the tall tales of Babs Cartland – God rest her pink soul – there's still a huge market for happy ever after. Readers insist on it. And, while I like a fruity bonkbuster as much as the next girl, I'm struck by how few novels tell the truth about love. Literature and poetry have the potential to enlighten us about love in all its forms, and yet most of us never venture beyond the bestsellers.

> **While I like a fruity bonkbuster as much as the next girl, I'm struck by how few novels tell the truth about love.**

So what's a girl to do? If you want to get a better idea about what really makes men and women tick, one of the most useful things you can do is to open your eyes to a wider worldview about relationships. Start reading a broader range of books, not just romantic novels. What do the classics or famous poets have to say about love? Read books written from a guy's perspective. Look at magazines and newspapers with a more critical eye. Go outside of your comfort zone – choose TV programmes and films that might offer a different take on the usual romantic popcorn. See what philosophy, counselling and psychology have to say about adult relationships. Buy other self-help books, dare I say it. Talk to people in successful relationships. Find out what they've got to say.

You'll get lots of conflicting advice but that's half the fun. Knowledge is power, especially when it comes to finding Mr Right. Who knows, you might start to see that some of your relationship 'truths' turned out to be make-believe after all…

• • •

3

Chapter Three

THE FIVE WORST MISTAKES WOMEN MAKE

...

Have you ever dated Prince Charming and then slowly, magically, inexplicably he transforms, before your very eyes, from a perfectly good prince into a hopping, croaking frog?

You can't believe your bad luck. It's like some kind of reverse alchemy – just when you thought you were getting somewhere, your golden boy turns back to into dating doo-doo.

What the hell happened? He seemed like one of life's nice guys. Well, maybe he was. And maybe he'd just had enough. If you're really honest with yourself, could it be something *you* did which brought the relationship crashing to its knees? Perhaps it's time to look at the five worst mistakes we women make to understand why they're so deadly in the world of dating.

• NO MORE MR NICE GUY? •

The first thing to say is that you can't suddenly turn a nice guy into a nasty one, unless you do something truly unforgivable. People's personalities might be malleable, but it's very difficult to change someone's moral core. The ten types of frogs in Chapter 1, for example, aren't horrible because princesses *make* them like that – saying that absolves frogs from any kind of responsibility. What is true, however, is that people, even nice ones, often treat you the way you let them.

In all kinds of social situations, you need to teach people how to treat you. As an adult, it's up to you to be clear about the way you want people to relate to you and this naturally extends into any romantic relationships. Do you want to be treated with respect? Do you expect loyalty and compassion from your partner? Would you like to be given the physical and emotional freedom to be yourself? I should think you do … but have you ever said it out loud?

• READ THE INSTRUCTIONS • CAREFULLY

When you buy a new car or television, you get a set of instructions. It's such a shame people don't come with the same. Wouldn't life be so much easier if, on the first date, you handed over a comprehensive instruction list of your likes and dislikes, personality quirks, expectations and desires? Your bloke could do the same. Rather than spend the next few months flailing around in dating darkness, you'd both have a much better idea of how you'd like to be treated.

Life isn't like that, of course, but there's something to be said for giving some thought about what you would write in your own 'owner's manual'. Whether you're in the throes of a relationship or taking time out, why not make a list of the ways you'd like to be treated in a loving relationship? Write it down if you want. Do you want your bloke to be honest with you? Do you expect him to be considerate and caring? Is it important that he has self-control and tolerance? What about traits such as generosity, politeness, reliability and friendship?

This list is important for two reasons. Firstly, when you find yourself lost in the middle of a tumultuous relationship, it can be sobering to look back at your instruction list and be reminded of the things that mattered to you. It's an eye-opener when you realise that your current relationship is falling short and it might give you the courage to ask for better.

The second reason is that relationships are a two-way street. You'll never be someone's princess if you're behaving like a witch, or indeed a scullery maid. You must treat your partner how you want them to treat you, so get your ideas clear before you start and keep asking yourself whether you're living up to your side of the bargain.

• MISTAKE 1: DESPERATION IS THE • WORST COLOGNE

It follows from this that certain types of behaviour will inevitably create problems in a relationship, however promising the prince. You can side-step all the frogs in the world, but if you keep committing relationship suicide, there'll never be a happy ending. So what are the five worst mistakes that women make? Mistake number one – being desperate.

Isn't it off-putting when someone tries too hard to sell you something? They might catch your attention initially but soon their sales pitch begins to sound desperate. But it's half price! Offer ends today! Get two for the price of one! The more discounts they offer, the less appealing the product sounds. You think to yourself: if the product is so great, why are they trying so hard? There must be something wrong with it. Nine times out of ten you walk away, suspicious because it's too cheap.

Relationships are the same. If you go into a relationship desperate for love, you'll sell yourself short. If you feel desperate, chances are you'll project that desperation. If you do all the running, there's no chase to be had. It's human nature that if something is easy to obtain, we don't want it. Do you really want to be a relationship bargain bin?

It's human nature that if something is easy to obtain, we don't want it.

So how do you know when you're being desperate? Ask yourself some questions:

- Are you looking for Mr Right or are you simply looking for Mr You'll Do?
- Are you becoming less discerning about who you date?
- Has your relationship wish-list been whittled down to 1) male; 2) detectable pulse?
- Has being alone got so tedious that you're starting to think that anyone would do?

If you feel yourself sliding into this category, don't panic.

STOP MAKING THE SAME MISTAKE ...

There are lots of things you can do to nip this nasty habit in the bud. The first is to stop wondering if every relationship is *the one*. By being a bit more relaxed and open-minded about each new date, you take the pressure off yourself. There's less at stake, so you can afford to be breezy.

The second trick is to stop trying to sell yourself on every date. People who divulge too much information or spend too long on self-promotion exude desperation. You'll also seem like you're trying way too hard to impress, a classic sign of insecurity. And it's pretty unappealing to have someone talk incessantly about themselves for two hours. Remember that being a good listener is one of the things human beings find most attractive in another person.

At the beginning of a relationship, it's important to unpeel yourself slowly and give your date a chance to talk about his own experiences and interests. Genuine intimacy takes time to develop. Equally, don't waste valuable time putting yourself down. Drawing attention to your insecurities isn't going to win you any prizes – are you really going to rely on the sympathy vote as a pulling strategy?

And do yourself a favour. On the first few dates, try to limit how much you bitch about your ex-boyfriend. He might have been a shit and had a small willy but endlessly slagging him off will only make you sound bitter.

You might also want to avoid talking about how much you'd like to get married and how you've already planned the big day down to bridesmaids' dresses and first dance song. And definitely don't share with him the top-ten baby names you've already picked out. While you're busy working out whether you prefer Grace or Honor for a girl, your hot date will have run screaming for the hills, leaving only a man-shaped hole in the wall.

• MISTAKE 2: BEING AN • EMOTIONAL LIMPET

Ever been in a relationship where you were compulsively texting, emailing or calling him? Did you constantly demand declarations of love or compliments? Did you make him feel guilty for wanting to spend time by himself or with friends? Did you spend most of the time feeling needy and insecure? Do you feel terror when he hasn't called for an hour? Are you analysing everything he says and does?

If a bloke has to prise your fingers from his ankles when he wants to leave the house, it's never a good sign. Behaving like an emotional limpet is not only degrading for you, and annoying for him, but it's guaranteed to put a death sentence on your hopes for long-term happiness. That's why it's mistake number two.

Nothing can thrive in such a suffocating atmosphere. Relationships need space and time to grow – how can this happen if you keep digging it up to see if it's flourishing? You'll kill the relationship stone dead. We all need extra reassurance now and again, but if you constantly behave like a demanding child, it's no wonder you've struggled to find Mr Right. In these kinds of relationships, the dynamic often gets worse over time rather than better. The more you act like a demanding clingy toddler, the more your prince will withhold his affection. You feel worse and demand more. He refuses to be bullied into showing affection and withdraws even further.

STOP MAKING THE SAME MISTAKE ...

You need to ask yourself why you are clingy. If it's because you don't really trust your partner, you have two choices. Both involve tackling the problem head on. If you don't trust your partner because he's inherently untrustworthy and has proved this over and over again, it's time to stop punishing yourself with an inadequate relationship and move on. If the trust issues lie with you and your insecurities, you need to find out what's causing them. Perhaps someone important in your past broke your trust? It needn't have been a boyfriend or a recent event. The old adage of 'once bitten, twice shy' can make you very suspicious of people's motives, even if they've given you no reason to doubt them. Resolving these issues, either by talking to friends and family, or through the skills of a professional counsellor, will help you feel more secure and move forward.

Boredom and loneliness can also make us clingy and insecure in a relationship. A common time for this to arise is when one partner is either unemployed, stuck at home, or feeling frustrated with their life. We begin to resent our partner's freedom and success. We feel left behind. Rather than getting validation from the outside world, we expect our partners to be able to make us feel confident and valuable again. But it's too much pressure to put on one person.

If you feel that might be happening in your relationship, the quickest way to solve it is to take up activities that make you feel good about yourself, whether it's socialising, work or hobbies. Christ, even line dancing is better than sitting on your arse doing nothing (although only just). Relationships work best when you can combine shared interests with independent lives, careers and friendships. Living vicariously through your partner's life isn't anyone's idea of perfect love.

• MISTAKE 3: SCREAM IF YOU • WANNA GO FASTER!

Think about roller-coaster rides for a minute. Thrill-seekers love them because they enjoy the element of risk that comes when you strap yourself in for a wild ride. The sheer freedom, terror and exhilaration you experience is a stark contrast to daily life, which can often feel stressful or overly structured.

But people do get hooked on the chemical effect that experiencing a rapid range of emotions can have. One minute you're screaming with fear, the next you're laughing hysterically. Not everyone enjoys these feelings but plenty do. That explains why some people never want to go on a roller-coaster again, while others don't want to get off them.

Dating can be the same. Some women thrive on the stress and upset that comes with a rocky relationship. The constant breaking up and making up. The screaming matches followed by sensational sex. The stormings off, slamming doors and weeping into pillows. Heady stuff but absolutely no recipe for a lasting relationship and definitely mistake number three. And here's why.

Being out of control emotionally will leave you exhausted in the long term. Just as you can't ride a roller-coaster for the rest of your life, neither can your body or mind stand the turmoil of a troubled relationship. And while it can feel wonderfully romantic to be constantly experiencing heightened emotions, there's no way you'll be able to sustain that for any length of time. If your relationship absorbs all your energies, there'll be nothing left for career, health, family and friendships.

Long-term, if you're thinking about settling down and having children, it's vital that you're in control of your emotions. You and your partner have a huge responsibility to provide a safe, secure, non-volatile environment for your kids. Your choices and behaviour will have a direct effect on them. If your offspring start to be affected by your amateur dramatics, suddenly all the endless cat fights and cuddling will start to look a bit shabby.

STOP MAKING THE SAME MISTAKE ...

Many people who end up in volatile relationships are often drawn to their self-destructive patterns. Remember the Empty Bowl style of parenting from Chapter 2? If you've grown up in a neglectful or unresponsive household, you may never have been taught how to manage your emotions in a rational, grown-up way. Either that or you find your partner's unpredictable affection almost comforting in its familiarity. Perhaps your family was akin to the Permissive Parenting style in the same chapter, and you're still struggling with the idea that you can't always get your own way?

Sometimes people get hooked on the sheer drama of a rocky relationship. If the rest of your life is unfulfilling or unexciting, it's no surprise that you might feel tempted to create a stir in your love life. Love is never felt more acutely than when you feel you're about to lose it.

Sometimes people get hooked on the sheer drama of a rocky relationship.

Unless you're prepared to spend the rest of your life in romantic limbo, however, you need to knock this nasty habit on its head. If your outbursts tend to be explosive, it might be worthwhile learning some basic anger management techniques (see Chapter 6 for tips on arguing and anger). Keeping your cool will stop minor disagreements turning into shouting matches.

If, on the other hand, you suspect that you are drawn to volatile relationships because you're frightened of intimacy or acting out self-destructive behaviour, it could be time to talk things through with a third party. You might not even know what's behind your behaviour – a trained counsellor can gently tease out answers and help you stop history repeating itself.

• MISTAKE 4: OOOH, BUT HE'S • GORGEOUS

Ever dated a man with the face of a model and the mind of a mange-tout? Did he sport a six-pack but struggle to string a sentence together? Dating a guy on looks alone is shamelessly shallow but, according to evolutionary biology, might not be entirely your fault. Plenty of research studies have found that certain physical characteristics that we'd typically call 'good-looking' are, in fact, universally attractive. We ladies, it seems, are irresistibly drawn to guys with masculine, angular faces, larger jaws and greater muscle mass. All of these traits suggest higher levels of testosterone in a bloke – a quality our distant, and distinctly hairier, prehistoric ancestors would have taken as a sign of good mating potential. A simple case of 'your cave or mine?'

> Ever dated a man with the face of a model and the mind of a mange-tout?

We also equate good looks with certain personality traits, even if the bloke in question doesn't actually have them. It's called the 'halo-effect' and numerous experiments have shown that women assign positive attributes to handsome men, even if they're total losers in real life. On looks alone, it seems that ladies presume that good-looking guys earn more money (about 12 per cent on average), are happier, more popular and less likely to commit a crime. A chilling piece of research by the University of Oslo, for example, found that recommended punishments for handsome burglars were 24 per cent lower than for your average-looking thief. For more serious crimes, such as manslaughter and rape, the advised sentences were about 10 per cent lighter. It seems as if good-looking guys can get away with murder, literally.

I'm certainly not saying that every handsome fellow is a Ted Bundy waiting to happen, but it's interesting that we ladies give cute guys more credit than they deserve. Which is possibly why dating on looks alone is so treacherous. We're so dazzled by beauty that we'll fail to see what's staring us in the face. Namely, that this person is not funny, smart or nice enough to be considered long-term material. Or, they might be all of these things and still not compatible. And, even when things are clearly going nowhere, we hang on for grim death because we can't face losing such a superficially perfect partner.

And spare a thought for the poor guy. Doesn't he deserve someone who loves him for his personality as well as his six-pack? He might be a really kind, sensitive and loving bloke underneath all those chiselled good looks and buff physique. And here you are simply using him for his fine features and scrummy body, you little minx.

STOP MAKING THE SAME MISTAKE ...

You'd think that the solution to this problem was to only go out with ugly men. The theory behind this is that, if your bloke is more chipmunk than Chippendale, he'll be so grateful to date you that he'll behave like the perfect gentleman, try incredibly hard in bed and treat you like a princess.

Don't be fooled. Dating someone who looks like a dog's dinner is as shallow as dating a dish. In both instances you're going on appearances rather than character. It's time to stop skimming the surface and make a serious attempt to date someone for their personality not their physique. Yes, you've got to find them attractive (see Chapter 5 for more about the importance of sexual chemistry), but there's also got to be something more substantial to the relationship. In a long-term relationship you soon get used to how the other person looks on the outside. It's not that you stop fancying them or appreciating their attractiveness – but, rather like a beautiful painting that hangs on your wall, you simply stop noticing their looks half so much. Other traits also become much more important. The more you know someone and like who they are and what they stand for, the more attractive they become. My husband looks no different from the day I met him and yet I'm much more attracted to him now than I was when we started out. That doesn't mean I didn't have the phwoar factor when we first dated – I certainly did – but I only became totally smitten when I knew more about what made him tick.

• MISTAKE 5: IS THERE ANYONE • HOME?

Just as desperation is the worst cologne, it seems that women can't resist the allure of *Eau d'Indifference*. It's a sad fact, but emotionally unavailable men are utter lady-magnets. The more they resist, the harder we try. The cooler they behave, the giddier we become. We girls love a challenge but there's something self-destructive about pursuing a relationship with someone who can't, or won't, meet you halfway. And that's why it's mistake number five.

So what defines an emotionally unavailable man? It could be a case of right guy, wrong time. Not necessarily a frog, just a prince in an emotional pickle. He might be Mr Rebound. He might be Mr Grieving. He might just be Mr Mixed-up. Whatever he is, he isn't in the right place to start a relationship. With anyone.

Or maybe, just maybe, you are Miss Wrong and he's not brave enough to tell you. You hang on to the hope that one day he'll wake up and realise that you're the love of his life. You keep telling yourself that because it's what you so desperately want. You're more than welcome to try and sit it out, but you could be in for a very long wait.

Or he could be wrong guy, wrong time. Someone who's never going to come up trumps, however long you wait. He might be emotionally unavailable because he's twigged that it makes women keen. He might already be married or have a girlfriend. In which case, he's a player. Great. Or, he might be unavailable because he simply hasn't got the emotional skills or time for a committed relationship. Double great.

So what's the appeal? Some women love to test themselves. Dating an emotionally unavailable man is like climbing Everest with your flip-flops on. Very few succeed and those who do are almost broken in the process. For some women, an emotional cripple brings out their nurturing side. They feel that with enough love, patience and effort, they can transform anyone into perfect boyfriend material. Others of us are so used to *not* getting what we need from a relationship that we begin to think it's all we deserve. So entering a relationship with an emotionally unavailable man simply confirms what we already believe about ourselves.

> ## Dating an emotionally unavailable man is like climbing Everest with your flip-flops on.

STOP MAKING THE SAME MISTAKE...

So how do you bypass this particular temptation? The first thing you need to do is to establish why you go for emotionally unavailable men. Maybe you should consider whether you're subconsciously opting for unsuitable men to sabotage any possibility of a loving, and therefore potentially risky, relationship? Are you really avoiding putting your heart on the line? Perhaps you don't think you deserve long-term happiness or don't think it's possible? It's time to find out why you're picking men who don't want you.

Think back to the idea of the 'owner's manual' at the beginning of this chapter. Ask yourself questions about what you really want from a relationship. Imagine what it would look and feel like. Imagine how it would pan out in 1, 10, 50 years' time. Now ask yourself, is Mr Unavailable ever going to fulfil my wish-list? Thought not.

• • •

4

Chapter Four

PRINCE CHARMING CAN KISS MY @***!

...

So, you've split up? Well, isn't that just great? All that time, effort and emotional investment gone straight down the plug hole. It makes you wonder why you bothered in the first place.

There is absolutely nothing funny about getting your heart trampled on. And yet, God bless us, most of us eventually pick ourselves up, dust ourselves off and get back in the ring. But how soon is *too* soon?

This is a book about finding Prince Charming and yet this chapter is all about avoiding relationships. Sometimes it's good to recognise when you need to take a break from dating. Perhaps you're just not in the right frame of mind. Perhaps you're in danger of a rebound relationship. Perhaps you're still pining for a lost love. Or maybe you just need time to realise that stalking your ex is more likely to get you a restraining order than a romantic reunion.

Sometimes you just need a breather. A rest is as good as a holiday, especially when it comes to dating. If you've just come out of a relationship, it's important to give yourself the emotional and physical space to take stock. You need time to assess what went wrong and, equally, what went right.

If you think that you don't need a break because the relationship was just another fling, perhaps it's time you asked yourself why you've become a serial dater. Are you dating to distract yourself from solving something that's been bothering you or to make you feel temporarily better about yourself?

• FIVE SIGNS YOU NEED A BREAK •
FROM BLOKES

1 **'All men are the same'.** If you hear yourself constantly slagging off the opposite sex, it's time to get a grip. Starting every new relationship with such low expectations is unfair to your partner and bound to become a self-fulfilling prophecy.

2 **Same girl, different frog.** Everyone has a 'type', but are you sure you're not going for the same frog time and time again? If every relationship ends with a croak, it's time to take yourself off the circuit and assess what's behind your bad choices.

3 **Whatsisname?** Nothing kills the moment like calling out the wrong name. If you find yourself cycling through the alphabet or resort to calling every boyfriend 'Darling', it suggests your brain can't keep up with your bonking.

4 **Overbooking.** 9.00am Jeff – coffee. 11.30am Chris – cinema. 3.00pm Bob – quick fumble. 7.00pm Sam – snog and snooze. Is your diary is starting to look more like an endless list of appointments? If you've got no time left for friends, family and fun, you're definitely in danger of over-dating.

5 **Talking about your ex.** Whether you're constantly mudslinging or missing him terribly, if you can't stop talking about your ex it's time to accept you're not quite ready for a new relationship. Give yourself time and try again later.

• BOING! THE BOUNCY WORLD • OF REBOUNDS

So what happens if you don't take a break from dating? One of the biggest dangers is that you'll fall into a rebound relationship – either with someone completely unsuitable or with someone who'll never have your full attention and commitment.

I have a confession to make. I met my husband only weeks after separating from my ex. Hypocritical, *moi*? Well, perhaps a bit. But I'm also keen to point out that meeting someone so soon after the devastating break-up of my first marriage was not the easiest route to take. Although it's all worked out in the end, I certainly wouldn't recommend it as a dating strategy. You'll see why in a minute.

So how do you know when a rebound is a rebound? There's no set time limit you should leave between boyfriends but there's a good chance you're not over your last love if you can tick these three boxes:

☐ Your ex still occupies your thoughts on a daily basis.

☐ When you think of him you feel overwhelmingly strong emotions whether it's upset, regret, guilt or longing.

☐ You still feel as if there are questions about the relationship you want answered.

Lots of people satisfy one of these conditions, myself included, but it's the unique combination of all three which signals that you're not emotionally ready for a new relationship. You may still think of your ex on a regular basis but if those thoughts are not accompanied by deep feelings or a strong desire to pick at your emotional scars, it's a promising sign that you've moved on.

The problems with rebound relationships are numerous. First, you rarely make a good judgement call when you're in the middle of an emotional crisis. Being stressed or upset often forces you to make rash decisions you'll regret later. It's the dating equivalent of shopping for a perfect outfit in a 10-minute lunch break – once in a while you might find the ideal dress but most of the time you're so rushed, you end up buying something that doesn't fit, costs too much and looks like you've fallen into a pair of curtains. Not good.

Rebound relationships are comparable to putting a sticking plaster on a broken leg. Throwing yourself into the arms, or bed, of another man will feel great temporarily but won't mend the underlying heartbreak. There's only so long you'll be able to bottle up your feelings and before you know it your new bloke will be faced with an emotional time-bomb on two legs. Kaboom!

Not only is this hugely unfair on the bloke in question – dealing with the emotional fallout from a previous relationship is a thankless task, just ask my husband – but it doesn't give the new relationship a proper chance to thrive. Every minute you spend thinking about your past relationship is a minute you could have spent focusing on your new one. Like a lovelorn Jacob Marley, you're dragging along cumbersome emotional chains forged in your last relationship. They're a heavy burden for any new relationship to carry.

Perhaps most of all, you're not being fair to yourself. When you come out of a relationship you're often bruised and battered, a shadow of your usual sparkly self. Or, it can go the other way and you cultivate a hard-nosed, don't-give-a-shit attitude, which equally doesn't do you justice. If you meet someone now, they're getting a hugely distorted view of your personality. There is an argument that if a bloke can love you when you're at your worst, then things can only get better. And there's some truth in that. The fact that my now husband could love me, even when there was lots of wailing and gnashing of teeth coming from my direction, helped me to trust that his feelings were real. However, it was a huge burden to place on his shoulders and I'm still amazed that he stayed the course.

The danger, however, is that you end up dating someone who only knows the rebound you. What's worse, they may even prefer this version to your real self. As soon as you stop being all vulnerable and needy, or being a ruthless tease, there's no guarantee that he'll like what's left behind. Only when you're back to normal will you really establish whether he likes the real, confident, independent you. And, more to the point, whether you actually like him.

• THE JOY OF SINGLEDOM •

Enough gloom. Forget rebound relationships for a moment and let's look at why being single is so central to becoming a well-rounded, open-hearted, non-bunny-boiling partner in the future.

Periods of singledom are a prime opportunity to get to grips with who we really are, what we want and where we're heading.

The best lessons we learn about love are when we're single. Relationships are often so all-consuming that we rarely get a chance to stop, think and reassess where we are. Periods of singledom are a prime opportunity to get to grips with who we really are, what we want and where we're heading.

It can be difficult, however, to see the bright side of being single when you've just had your heart ripped out. But this in itself is another reason to delay diving into a new relationship – the end of a significant love can be as traumatic as bereavement and you need to grieve before you can attempt to start again.

• HOW A BROKEN HEART HEALS • ITSELF

It might seem a bit overdramatic to compare the end of a relationship to the death of a loved one, but anyone who's had their heart broken will know how apt the analogy is. In fact, relationship counselling often compares the pain of heartbreak to the pain of bereavement, as in both cases the sufferer often goes through similar feelings and behaviours.

It's important to understand and recognise each stage of recovery from heartbreak. Working backwards, the best relationships are those between people who've spent plenty of time enjoying being single. And being happily single is only possible when you've fully recovered from the pain of a previous break-up.

So what are the stages of a heart mending itself? And how will you recognise that this process is complete so you can start making the most of being single and, eventually, if you want, finding your Prince Charming?

Okay. Let's start at the moment the relationship ends. (You might not experience all these five stages, or some may affect you more profoundly than others, but you'll get the general gist.)

1 **The *'This Isn't Happening to Me'* stage**
Also known as the denial stage, this tends to be a relatively brief phase where you refuse to accept the truth that the relationship is over, or you attempt to minimise its importance. You might feel numb, calm or even strangely light-hearted. Your brain has triggered this reaction in response to news that is simply too hard for you to accept at that moment. Even the most rational of us can behave oddly at this stage – whether it's keeping the split a secret or stalking your ex. Shock can make us do funny things.

2 **The *'What a Total Bastard'* stage**
Pretty soon you start to face the reality of the situation and anger kicks in. Life seems unfair; everyone else is happy except you; how dare other couples be in love; and, most of all, how could he do this to YOU? You're in immense pain and it's sometimes easier to be angry than upset. You may even start plotting some kind of revenge in the hope that it will make you feel better. This tends to be the 'cutting up his suits/trashing his car/sewing prawns into the curtains' stage.

3 **The *'I'll Do Anything to Get Him Back'* stage**
As the anger wears off, you're left with the cold hard truth
that you're on your own. It's at this stage that many people
resort to bargaining – attempting to restart the relationship
on any terms, even ones that seem desperate. You promise
to be a better girlfriend. You offer to accept his infidelities.
You beg to have him back, even if he can't give you what
you want. (This is a key time when warring couples give
it another go, despite the fact that one side has effectively
relinquished all their power. Not a good basis for long-
term success as all the old resentments soon flare up.)

4 **The *'Everything Reminds Me of Him'* stage**
This is where things get tough. You've finally realised
that you're not going to get back together and the only
way forward is to wade through weeks or months of
sadness. Stock up on tissues because there's bound to be
lots of weeping and wailing. Every song/chick flick/crisp
wrapper will remind you of him. Your friends will get a
bad case of sympathy fatigue as you analyse the minutiae
of your relationship. But hang in there, because this is
the most important stage of getting over someone and,
once you've been through it, you'll have put some much-
needed emotional miles between you and your ex.

5 **The *'Thawing Out'* stage**
This last stage is one of acceptance. Acceptance that the
relationship is over and acceptance that it's time to get on
with the rest of your life. Dating other people probably
seems like a step too far at this stage – everything is too raw
– but now is a good time to start thinking about how you're
going to exploit this new single life to its full potential.

• SQUEEZING EVERY LAST DROP OUT • OF BEING SINGLE

There are moments in single life when you feel about as wanted as a fart in an elevator. It probably feels like everyone is in a couple apart from you. Everyone's loved up and having babies. There's no-one to give you a late-night cuddle, pour you a glass of fizzy or mend your shower when it breaks. Your sex life has virtually dried up and you're even beginning to wonder if there's any point bleaching your moustache.

When you feel like that, it can be hard to remember what's so great about being single. But let me remind you. Not only is it one of the only times in your entire life when you can do, be, say and behave exactly the way you want to, it's also an unmissable opportunity to find out what you *really* want from life and love. Draw up your life plan. Plot your next moves. Change direction if that's what you need. Demand better for yourself. It's like taking a career-break without the pay cut.

DISCOVER WHAT MAKES YOU HAPPY. Use this time to follow your own passions and pursuits with unbridled enthusiasm. So much of being in a relationship involves compromise – it's easy to lose sight of what matters to you, especially if you're trying to fit in with someone else's lifestyle. Use this time to try new sports or hobbies. Take up waterskiing. Learn to make sausages. Become a black belt in origami.

FIND OUT WHAT YOU REALLY WANT FROM A PARTNER. Remember the relationship wish-list you read about in Chapter 3? Now's the time to write your 'owner's manual'. Think about what you want from a partner. How would he treat you? What would he be like? How would you feel in a relationship with him? The great thing about doing this list when you're single is that you're not constantly trying to make your current partner fit your requirements. Start with a blank canvas. Aim high.

> ## Now's the time to write your 'owner's manual'. Think about what you want from a partner.

VISUALISE WHAT YOUR FUTURE COULD HOLD. Think about the life that you want for yourself in 1, 5, 10, 30 years' time. What does it look like? Who does it involve? Are children in the equation? Do you want to be married? Does being single actually fit better with your life plan? Think about the places you'd like to see and the things you want to achieve. Where will you be in your career? Is money, security, freedom important? Visualising these future events can help you plan how you're going to achieve these goals, whether it's through making new friends, changing jobs, retraining, or sorting out past issues that are holding you back.

RECONNECT WITH FAMILY AND FRIENDS. One of the sobering things about a break-up is that it can make you realise you've been neglecting friends and family. Use this time to build bridges and strengthen those ties. You can't make a romantic relationship the only source of social contact you have – it puts all your eggs in one basket and will leave you very isolated should you split up. You need your own network of support, one that is independent of any past or future boyfriends.

UNDERSTAND THE VALUE OF BEING INDEPENDENT. It's a cliché, but the best relationships work when a couple want to be together but don't *have* to be together. Your independence will be one of your most attractive qualities. Couples who cling together tend to drag each other down, often to the point where they can't function as separate entities. Do you really want to date someone who's only with you because they fear being on their own? Remember that bad relationships drain your energy. Good ones give you the freedom to fly.

PUT PAST RELATIONSHIPS IN CONTEXT. When the dust settles, use this time to reflect on your past relationships. What lessons can you learn? Do any patterns emerge? Can you get any closure? As the anger subsides, perhaps you'll start to see things more clearly. It's time to be brutally honest with yourself. What things will you do differently next time? If you can't seem to stop history repeating itself or you remain bewildered about what went wrong, think about working through these issues with a counsellor.

• GETTING BACK IN THE RING •

Some people decide that a single life is infinitely preferable to a long-term relationship. In a culture dominated by coupledom, you have to admire that kind of emotional self-reliance and independent spirit. But this is a book about finding love. You didn't pick up a copy just to be told 'have fun, stay single'. Now we understand the importance of time alone, let's get back to the task in hand.

Getting back into dating can be a bit scary when you're feeling bruised and battered. Your self-confidence might have taken a knock or maybe you feel like your small-talk skills are a bit rusty. Here are five quick tips to get you started:

1 CHOOSE THE RIGHT STAMPING GROUND. There's nothing more depressing than an evening spent propping up a bar, nursing a Woo Woo, in the vain hope that the man of your dreams will burst through the door. If you want to meet someone with similar interests to you, choose an event or place that's likely to attract them. If you're into art, join a drawing class or visit lots of galleries. If you're into the outdoors, tag onto a hiking club or volunteer for a conversation group. If you're into crown green bowls, hang around the local retirement home and bring along a packet of Rich Tea biscuits.

2 CREATE A WISH-LIST. There's no point starting a relationship with someone who's about to relocate to Ulan Bator. Keep an open mind by all means but there's absolutely no mileage in dating someone who is totally unsuitable or unavailable. Think back to the 'owner's manual' we talked about in Chapter 3. What kinds of traits really matter to you in a man? Are there any deal-breakers, such as not wanting kids or different religious or political views? You don't want to be too prescriptive but equally you want someone who at least ticks some of your boxes.

3 LOOK THE BUSINESS. You might be an absolute cracker on the inside, but if people keep throwing pennies at you in the street, there's a good chance it's time for a make-over. Get yourself a haircut, pick out your best rags (or, dare I say it, splash out on some new ones) and go out smelling of roses. There's no point adopting the attitude that he'll have to take you as he finds you – dating is about presenting yourself at your very best. Surely it's not too much to ask to give the poor bloke at least a few months of perfection before you revert back to hairy legs and yesterday's pants?

4 LEARN TO TALK. Nerves can wreak havoc with your usual conversational skills, so have some questions ready to help your date go smoothly (if you're really jittery you can write these down and swot up every time you pop to the loo). Imagine the conversation as a meal of three courses. The starter should be some general small talk to put your date at ease – the usual polite, non-personal questions such as "Did you have a good journey?" "Have you come far?" "Would you like a drink?" "Is there anything on the menu you can recommend?" and so on. The second course involves getting to know a bit more about your date but not getting too personal. "Tell me about your job", "What do you do in your spare time?", "Do you travel much?" The last part of the conversation, when you should both be feeling much more comfortable with each other, can be more philosophical or exploratory. Ask questions that reveal more about your date's hidden hopes and aspirations, views and opinions: "Is there anywhere you'd like to visit that you've not been to yet?", "Who, from history, would you like to meet?", "What did you want to be when you were little?", "Who do you admire?"

5 FIVE – BE SAFE. You don't need to smuggle a cattle-prod into your handbag but do follow some basic guidelines about personal safety. After all, you're meeting a stranger. Here are some do's and don'ts:

- Try to make the first few meetings at lunchtime. Not only is it guaranteed to be daylight but you're also less likely to cloud your judgement with booze.

- Meet in a public place – such as a restaurant or cinema – where it's easy for you to leave if you need to make a swift exit.

- Tell a friend where you are going and who you're going to meet.

- Make sure you have double-checked that the person is who they say they are. It's not always easy but you can check that they work for who they say they do; or get them to give you a landline number and call them at home before you meet.

- Arrange for your own transport to and from the date, and always take your mobile phone with you.

- Consider double-dating with another couple.

- And above all, trust your instincts.

5

Chapter Five

FIVE PERSONALITY TRAITS EVERY PRINCE SHOULD HAVE

...

Ask most girls in their late teens what they look for in a man and, in no particular order, you'll usually get the same reply: pots of money, good-looking, great body, large todger. And while I like the sound of all those attributes very much, I can also say with great confidence that none of these now makes it on to my top five character traits every prince should have.

If a prince just so happens to be rich, gorgeous and well-endowed, great. I mean, you don't want to look a gift horse in the mouth. But these traits should be the icing on the cake. As time goes on, and we get older, wiser and wobblier, most of us realise that the things that *really* matter in a long-term relationship have little to do with your bloke having lots of cash or a cute tush.

So what should you be looking for in Prince Charming? It's taken as read that he won't have any of the froggish traits outlined in Chapter 1. But what makes him good relationship material? And do looks and sexual chemistry matter in the slightest? We'll look at the second question later in the chapter. In the meanwhile, here's a quick look at some essential personality traits and why they're such deal breakers ...

• TRAIT 1: LOVING •

Dah ... yeah. Of course your prince should be loving. But have you ever thought about what you *really* mean when you say that? To borrow an idea from social psychologist Zick Rubin, romantic loving seems to involve three different factors – attachment, caring and intimacy. Let's take each of these elements in turn.

ATTACHMENT

What do we mean by attachment? Attachment at its most basic is affection or loyalty that links one person to another. In romantic relationships, there are four styles of attachment: secure, anxious-preoccupied, dismissive-avoidant, and fearful-avoidant. Only one of these styles – secure attachment – makes for a happy, long-term future. If you are securely attached to your partner, you feel confident about depending on him but also aware of the need to be an autonomous, self-reliant person. This is healthy. Well done you.

Anxious-preoccupied adults, on the other hand, crave dependency but don't feel able to function as an individual outside the relationship – say hello to the stereotypical clingy partner. Dismissive-avoidant people go the opposite way and want all the independence without any of the emotional closeness – you'd be forgiven for wondering why they bother with a relationship in the first place. And fearful-avoidant adults have the worst of both worlds – like a child with his nose pressed up against the sweet-shop window, they're desperate for the emotional connection and closeness of a healthy relationship, but feel too scared to go inside and make it happen.

CARING

So what about being caring? Why is that part of being a loving person? We are essentially selfish creatures. We like to get our own way. And yet valuing another person's happiness and wishes as much as your own is a vital part of being in a romantic relationship. Remember the idea about 'emotional porridge' from Chapter 2? People brought up by permissive parents, who catered to their every whim, often find this element of love the most difficult. If you're used to getting your own way all the time, it can be very hard to make the sacrifices needed to make someone else happy. But relationships are all about give and take. Sometimes you get your own way. Sometimes you don't. That's life. And the funny thing is, the more you love someone, the easier it is to put their needs before your own. Making them happy makes you happy. I'm not saying that being a doormat is a prerequisite for a fruitful relationship – we've seen in Chapter 1 what can happen when you date a frog who's a pushover. What is true, however, is that real love is about managing differences and desires so that *both* partners feel happy and fulfilled in the long run. That takes ongoing work and effort but it's also hugely rewarding Love is an activity, not just a feeling that washes over you.

INTIMACY

The final element to a loving relationship is intimacy. The word 'intimate' has come to have horrible associations with feminine freshness and panty liners. Or it can have slightly seedy overtones. The true meaning of the word, however, is about sharing your deepest, most profound thoughts and feelings with another person.

> **Love is an activity, not just a feeling that washes over you.**

Most of our lives are spent being different versions of ourselves. In the space of one day you can be a work colleague, a mum, a friend, a lover, a helpful stranger, a daughter and everything in between. But which is our most authentic self?

Chances are, a partner will know you better than anyone else. And that's the way it should be. They are the only ones who, as an adult, see you stripped naked, both emotionally and literally. True intimacy is about togetherness, belonging and closeness. If you can't share your innermost feelings with your partner, how can you ever truly know each other?

• TRAIT 2: HARDWORKING •

You might think it funny to have this trait so high on your list of priorities. What difference does it make whether your bloke has a good work ethic or not? It all sounds terribly old-fashioned doesn't it? And yet, ask any women in a stable, committed relationship – especially one where there's kids involved – and nine times out of ten they'll agree.

Don't get me wrong, being hard-working is not the same as being a workaholic. I've seen the effects of people who always put work before relationships and family and it never has a happy ending. But there's a huge difference between that, and living with someone who's putting all their energies into building a future, for the both of you.

Being hard-working doesn't just apply to a career path. The term has much broader implications. When I talk about a prince needing to be hard-working, what I really mean is that life is infinitely easier and more pleasurable if you've shacked up with someone who's prepared to put plenty of effort into making your lives work together. Whether that manifests itself in him being industrious at work, or whether he's fantastic at thinking of ways to spend quality time together, it all boils down to the same thing. If your relationship is a rowing boat, it's good to know that you're *both* pulling on the oars.

It's very reassuring to be with someone who doesn't bail out easily. Life throws up all kinds of nasty surprises – bereavement, unemployment, illness and so on – and it's great to know that your partner isn't the kind of person who's going to jump ship when the going gets tough. Even the most normal of life events can be excruciatingly stressful – marriage, babies, moving house. When the shit hits the fan, you suddenly realise the importance of being loved by someone who also knows how to persevere. There's nothing worse than a fair-weather fella.

• TRAIT 3: COMMITTED •

Ahhhh … the C-word. If you believe most romantic fiction, you'll be forgiven for thinking that most blokes run a mile from commitment. And yet that just isn't borne out in real life. Yes, some men are commitment phobic, but so are an equal number of women.

Most people actually like the idea of being committed to another person. In a recent study of British 16-24 year olds (an age group you'd think would figure lowest for long-term commitment), three-fifths still believe that marriage is 'a natural step in confirming your commitment', whilst less than one-fifth feel the idea is outdated. What's more, over half the adult population are currently married and that doesn't even include people who are in civil partnerships or co-habiting.

If you look commitment up in a dictionary, it says things like 'to pledge or bind oneself to an idea or person'. It also talks about being 'morally dedicated to a course of action' and even 'an obligation which restricts freedom of action'. Yikes.

It sounds scary but the wonderful thing about a committed relationship is that the other person has made the same pledge. Yes, it might be hard to comprehend the idea that, from now on, you can't just bonk whoever happens to cross your path. But the great thing is that your partner has promised to do the same. You've both bound yourself emotionally to each other and are prepared to do what it takes to make the relationship work. Commitment is easy when things are going well but the true test comes when times are tough. It's also the point at which you realise just how important being committed is.

On the flipside, it's a nightmare living with someone who won't commit to anything. So much of adult life is about long-term plans – buying a house, having kids, holding down a job. How can you make any far-reaching decisions if you don't know whether your bloke is even going to be around in a week's time? You can't. Nothing can progress without the mutual conviction that you're both going to stick around long enough to see things through to their natural conclusion. A relationship without commitment is like being stuck in permanent Groundhog Day. If you live only for the day, there's no room for tomorrow. (To find out how to spot the signs that your bloke is ready for commitment, check out Chapter 7: 'What makes Prince Charming commit?')

A relationship without commitment is like being stuck in permanent Groundhog Day.

• TRAIT 4: HONEST •

Sometimes you have to admire people who tell lies. Weaving a web of deceit is a time-consuming affair, one that requires a good memory, vivid imagination and no sense of shame. And yet, after reading about Mr Liar Liar in Chapter 1, we also know what a bugger it can be dating someone who can't separate fact from fiction.

We all lie from time to time – often to spare the feelings of a loved one or avoid a sticky situation. So how honest does a bloke need to be if he's going to be your knight in shining armour? You can't have a lie detector strapped to his soft bits for the entire relationship, so what's a realistic goal to aim for?

Sometimes it's kinder to tell a fib. This is a normal part of everyday etiquette – white lies help grease the wheels of social contact. When faced with the loaded gun that is "Does my bum look big in this?" only a bloke with a death-wish would say "Yes, darling, like a barrage balloon". Telling the absolute unvarnished truth can sometimes be hurtful and counter-productive in a relationship, so there's nothing wrong with a man who knows when to be diplomatic. There's a subtle art to knowing when your girlfriend is asking you to tell her the truth and when she simply wants confirmation that she's attractive/valued/appreciated. It's a relationship minefield and one that most of us get wrong occasionally.

We also tell lies to ourselves. Life is stuffed with risks, dangers and problems. If we thought about them too much, we'd struggle to get out of bed on a morning. Telling ourselves that nothing bad is going to happen may statistically be a lie, but it's a damned sight easier than going through life being crippled by fear.

So when does useful fibbing turn into malicious lying? What are the differences between a good and bad lie in a relationship? In a sense, it's less about the content of the lie and more about the motive. If your bloke makes a regular habit of the following, it's time to drop him like a hot potato:

- lying to hurt you and help nobody (the 'you're a fat pig' lie)

- lying to hurt you but help him (the 'everyone thinks I'm too good for you' lie)

- lying for the sole pleasure of deceiving you or covering his tracks (the 'of course I'm not having an affair' lie)

- lying to avoid a decision (the 'I need some time' lie)

- lying to avoid confrontation (the 'I'm just tired alright?' lie).

Relationships that work have to be based on honesty. Being honest about your intentions. Being honest about your feelings. And being honest about who you are. Only when you give someone the full facts can you be sure that they're with you for the right reasons. And, equally, only when you know the full measure of your partner can you decide whether he's the right man for you.

• TRAIT 5: RESPECTFUL •

In the dim and distant past the word 'respect' meant showing deferential regard for someone 'above' you – for example, respecting your elders, doffing your cap, etc. Nowadays, in the baggy-panted world of teen gangsta speak, respect has come to mean bullying other people into looking up to you, even if you do nothing to deserve their admiration. The kind of respect I'm talking about is nothing to do either of these extremes.

When I say that Prince Charming has to respect you, what I mean is that he needs to recognise and appreciate your worth. Your opinions should matter to him, whether he agrees with them or not. He should value your personal qualities and abilities, learn to love the similarities and differences between you both, and also trust you to get on with your life without feeling the need to interfere or intrude. Respect in a relationship is about listening to your loved one, without constantly feeling the need to interrupt or belittle. It's about taking your partner's feelings into consideration and trying to put yourself in their shoes. Respect means agreeing to disagree, whilst all the time keeping an open mind to new ideas. It means never bullying or guilt-tripping your partner into doing something they don't want to do. It also means knowing when to give them the space they need.

Phew. That's quite a list and even the most perfect couples don't always live up to these standards. The point is, however, that this is what you should be aiming for. And, more importantly, if you want respect from Prince Charming, you need to offer him the same courtesy in return. Respect goes both ways.

• DOES IT MATTER WHETHER YOU • WANT TO RIP HIS CLOTHES OFF OR NOT?

I want to say 'no' but I'd be a big fat liar. It doesn't matter if the rest of the world thinks your prince looks like a bulldog licking shit off a thistle – if you think he's gorgeous, that's all that counts. Sexual attraction comes in many guises and a guy doesn't have to be conventionally good-looking to be attractive to women. In fact, it seems as if he doesn't have to be good-looking at all. That's the beauty of love – there's a lid for every pot.

Saying that sexual chemistry matters is strangely counter-intuitive to everything women are taught about relationships. Time and time again we're told not to judge a book by its cover, it's what's on the inside that counts, good looks fade over time. All this is true and there is absolutely no way you should date a man on looks alone, unless all you want is arm-candy. But romantic relationships, in my humble opinion, do need that extra sparkle if they're going to be successful in the long run. That indefinable quality is the thing that separates a friendship from a relationship.

> There is absolutely no way you should date a man on looks alone, unless all you want is arm-candy.

So why is passion important? It seems that those tingles that we get when we fall in love (or lust) play an important part in the mating game. Like a delicious starter before a main meal, these giddy feelings whet our appetite for a longer, more fulfilling relationship which, in the long term, hopefully provides a stable environment in which to raise children.

An idea developed by eminent anthropologist, Dr Helen Fisher, explains the process as happening in three distinct stages. First you feel lust. Grrr. This emotion has evolved to encourage us to seek sexual relations with almost any half-decent prospect (hence being able to fancy lots of different kinds of men at one time). Once we've found someone we like, the next stage, romantic love, helps us focus all our energies onto this one person, rather than trying to bond with several different blokes at the same time. Once this stage is complete, feelings of long-term attachment kick in, making us feel calm and secure. It's this sense of security about our partner that encourages us to feel confident enough to start reproducing.

But does that mean that sexual chemistry stops being important after a few years of being together? Definitely not. We tend to separate the idea of being a devoted couple and being a sexual couple, as if somehow we expect our desire for lovemaking to decrease the more time we spend with our partners.

Admittedly, keeping your sex life fresh after being married for 40 years is no mean feat and there are hundreds of books dedicated to putting the oomph back in the bedroom. Sex changes in frequency and intensity over the years – try getting into the wheelbarrow position with a dodgy knee and a hip replacement. But that doesn't mean sexual contact becomes any less important.

Research has revealed that making love, orgasms, foreplay and even a good hug release a hormone called oxytocin. Nicknamed by biologists as the 'love potion', oxytocin has been linked to all kinds of emotions that we want to feel in relationships – intimacy, sexual receptiveness, being closely bonded with your partner. Oxytocin also increases your desire to have more physical contact – in other words, the more sex you have with your loved one, the more you'll want it again. It gets to the stage, argues psychologist Professor Diane Witt, that the release of oxytocin becomes so conditioned after repeatedly having sex with the same partner that just *seeing* your bloke releases more oxytocin, making you want to be with them even more. Good eh?

• FOREVER FRIENDS? •

It goes without saying that your partner should also be your best friend – someone you can trust with secrets, moan about your day with, and who doesn't mind if you hang about the house in tracky bums and greasy hair. But what about relationships that start with friendship? Are they doomed to fail? Not all of us feel lust for our partners when we first meet them. That doesn't mean you can never develop romantic feelings for them, it simply means that you haven't gone for your usual type of bloke. Pretty soon, however, you'll need that friendship to develop into romantic love or your relationship will feel sorely lacking.

Relationships that don't have a sexual side can work, but only if that's what you *both* want. What tends to happen, however, is that one partner comes to realise that actually it does matter. While you're happy to pootle along in your passionless relationship, you may wake up to find your loved one has packed his bags, bonked someone else or moved in with the nanny.

If you've met a great guy and you're not sure whether the chemistry is there, there are lots of things you can do to stoke the flames. Don't be ashamed to make a project of it. Read lots of books about improving sexual chemistry in a relationship. Rent lovers' guide DVDs to help you put the sizzle into your sex life. Talk to a sex therapist or couples counsellor either together or apart. Make time for intimacy – sometimes sexual chemistry hasn't developed simply because you've been too busy, stressed or tired. Talk to each other about what you want and hope for from your sex life – you might find that your partner has simply been waiting for you to give him the green light. Above all, don't be afraid to give it time. If, however, you're still plugging away after six months or a year, and raised not so much as a smile, it might be time to throw in the towel and accept that you were better at friendship than fondling.

• • •

6

Chapter Six

EVEN PRINCES AND PRINCESSES HAVE THEIR OFF-DAYS

...

How soon in a new relationship can you go for a poo in your boyfriend's toilet? How many months do you have to be together before it's okay to parp under the bed covers? And just when is it safe to revert back to grey baggy knickers after months of having your bottom cheese-wired by skimpy thongs?

We all try to make a good impression when we start dating a new bloke. And a large part of that is pretending that we're nothing less than perfect. As well as making a huge effort to be the wittiest, sexiest, most adorable woman alive, we also tend to avoid confrontation for fear that it will burst the honeymoon bubble.

Sooner or later, however, you'll have your first row. But don't feel bad. Actually, congratulate yourself on the fact that your relationship has gone one step further. Show me a couple who don't argue and I'll show you a couple who don't really know each other. Chances are, if you never row, it's because you never feel able to express yourself or you don't care enough to bother.

• DING DING ROUND ONE •

It's totally normal to argue. Some couples fight like cat and dog. Others talk things through slowly. What separates a healthy relationship from a harmful one is not whether you have arguments but how you behave when you row and what effect disagreements have on your relationship, which we'll take a look at later in the chapter.

But first, why do we argue? It seems incomprehensible to me that two people can share the same space for any length of time and not annoy each other eventually. When you get together with someone, you also take on their personality quirks, peculiar habits, neuroses and foibles. You also have to adopt their friends, work colleagues, family members and perhaps even a pet or two. And guess what? They get yours in return.

It would be an absolute miracle if you didn't find things about the other person that irritated you. Comedians make careers out of these battle-of-the-sexes anecdotes – loo seats left up, poor map reading, fights over the remote control – in fact they've become a tedious cliché. And yet, we're all secretly relieved to hear that other couples feel the same as we do.

Some arguments are about more serious things – money, kids, work, health, responsibility – and these tend to rear their heads more than once. Couples actually have the same arguments again and again over the course of a relationship. Like a broken record, partners who've been together for 10 years still row about the same narrow set of problems they had from the outset. My husband and I have a 'menu of quarrels' we always pick from, which includes: the *'You're Not Spending Enough Time With Our Daughter'* argument; the *'You're Working Too Hard and I Never See You'* argument; the *'That Bloody Dog'* argument and my personal seasonal favourite, the *'I Can't Live Without Central Heating Anymore'* argument.

And it seems we're not alone. A recent US study found that couples argued, on average, once every two days. Of the hundreds of things people in long-term relationships could potentially row about, five came out as favourites in a One Poll survey. These were, in order of frequency:

1 Saying the wrong thing

2 Taking each other for granted

3 Being unable to find something in the house

4 Disagreements about raising the children

5 Money.

I'd say that my husband and I tick all five boxes on a fairly regular basis, especially if we're both tired or stressed about something else.

Couples have the same arguments again and again.

Not only are rows normal, under the right conditions they can actually be beneficial. Sometimes it takes a real set-to to remind you that your partner is actually a separate person, with his own wishes and ways of doing things. A constructive argument can help you to see them in a fresh light or make you prioritise their changing needs. It can be all too easy to get swept up in the other parts of your life – work, kids, money and so on – and neglect the person sitting right next to you. A row can highlight that fact that it's time for a little relationship tweaking. Not only that, but the kissing and making up after an argument can be a delicious way to remind both of you just how much you mean to each other. The Americans call this 'peace-pipe sex' and it can help you reconnect emotionally when you find yourselves in two opposing camps. (Just make sure, however, that exciting make-up sex doesn't become the only grounds for intimacy.)

While it's helpful to reassure yourself with the knowledge that it's okay to argue, you can't just leave it there. You need to learn *how* to argue. Couples who bicker incessantly become bogged down with frustration and bitterness and don't stand a chance in the long run. You only have to look at the reasons that couples get divorced to know how important good communication skills are. While adultery and violence ended the majority of marriage in post-war Britain, the top reasons for filing for divorce in the 21st century are emotional factors such as non-communication and lack of attention.

If you've got kids, it's also important to learn how to resolve differences in a way that doesn't leave the rest of the family traumatised. Some parents try to hide arguments from their children and, while you can understand their motives, secret arguing can be detrimental in the long run. Shielding children from every tiny disagreement can lead to them having a warped view about how adults deal with difficult emotions such as anger. Kids need to learn how to handle conflict and resolve difference without resorting to violence or name-calling. They also need to know that disagreements don't have to mean the end of a relationship.

Research by Cardiff University backs up this idea. In a three-year study, they found that it was better to argue in front of children than hide arguments, as long as the rows were constructive, discussion-type arguments, which came to some kind of resolution at the end. Problems arose when the arguments either came to no resolution or, even worse, when parents launched into destructive or violent slagging matches. There's also a definite list of topics that you shouldn't argue about in front of kids – adult topics such as sex or infidelity are definitely not appropriate, as are disagreements about parenting styles or problems with the children themselves.

Chronic arguing also damages kids. Research by the US National Institute of Mental Health found that parents whose angry clashes go on for years create a horrible emotional climate, which interferes with a child's normal psychological development. Kids raised in these environments tend to switch off emotionally, lose interest in their surroundings, and swing between being withdrawn and spontaneous angry outbursts. It just goes to show how important it is to get arguing right.

HOW NOT TO ARGUE

So what is the best way to handle your differences? While some couples seem to think that the best way to air their grievances is to go on daytime TV and scream bloody-murder, there are, not surprisingly, more effective ways to deal with conflict. But first, let's look at ways to get it wrong. Welcome to 'How Not To Argue':

● **Silent treatment** – *"Talk to the hand cause the face ain't listening"*
Sulking or sending your partner to Coventry might
make you feel powerful in the short term but maintaining
a wall of silence will only delay getting the problem solved.

● **Denying there's a problem** – *"Stop making a fuss, it's no big deal"*
If you constantly refuse to accept there's a problem,
eventually your partner will stop trying to sort things out.
A relationship where one half has effectively given up has
a very limited shelf-life.

● **Getting defensive** – *"That's rich coming from you"*
Attack may be the best form of defence on the battlefield

but it's an absolute no-no in relationships. Defending yourself by diverting attention back onto your partner will only confuse the issue at hand.

- **Guilt-tripping** – *"How can you do this to me?"*
  Making your partner feel terrible for raising an issue in the relationship is a nasty trick to play. If it matters to him it should matter to you, regardless of how difficult it may be to hear.

- **Getting third-party support** – *"Your mother says you're lazy too"*
  No-one likes being ganged up on. Your gripe is between the two of you – trying to garner support from friends, family or, even worse, your kids, will only alienate your partner and cause divisions.

- **Generalising** – *"You always do this"*
  Stick to the argument in hand. Making sweeping generalisations about a partner's behaviour, based on a few isolated incidents, will make him feel attacked and force him to go on the defensive. Absolutes such as 'always' and 'never' are rarely true.

- **Going for the Achilles heel** – *"My last boyfriend never did this"*
  Everyone has their weak spot. Attacking a partner by drawing attention to the thing they feel most worried or anxious about is a dirty tactic. Make sure you don't say anything you can't take back.

- **Ranting and raging** – *"Well f**k you then, I'm off"*
  Screaming, shouting, tantruming – the emotional strategy of a toddler. It's not big and it's not clever. In fact, it can

be downright scary for your other half and is no way for a grown-up to behave.

- **Verbal and physical violence** – *"You're a useless bitch"*
Personal insults, threats, bullying, intimidation, physical violence. Don't even think about it.

• HOW TO ARGUE •

Doesn't it feel great when you win an argument? You've floored your opponent with an intellectual left hook and he's out for the count. As you walk away punching the air and uttering the words "Eat shit loser", you feel as puffed up as a pigeon and ready to take on the next foolhardy challenger. (Or is that just me?) Pretty soon, however, something starts to niggle. Doubts creep in. Did I play fair? Have I been too mean? Did he really deserve such a thrashing?

How do you end an argument with a win/ win situation?

From a young age we're taught to be competitive at arguing. Arguments are battles. One person wins. One person loses. It's a fight to the death. And yet this approach is totally counter-productive in a healthy relationship. When it comes to love, both parties need to come out of an argument believing that their feelings have been validated and their opinions heard. With so many different views to accommodate, how do you end an argument with a win/win situation?

RIGHT TIME, RIGHT PLACE

Find a quiet place, somewhere where you both feel comfortable and are unlikely to be disturbed, e.g. not in a packed restaurant or over the phone at work. Give the other person your full attention and resist the urge to do another activity at the same time (how annoying is it when you're trying to talk to someone who's busy texting for example?). Same goes for washing up, driving, checking emails and so on. Make sure you don't have to be somewhere else soon or you risk leaving the argument unresolved. And make sure you're not too tired, stressed or distracted – one of the biggest relationship myths is 'don't go to bed on an argument'. If you're absolutely knackered and you know you're not thinking straight, leave things to the morning.

DIP YOUR TOE IN

Don't launch into a full-scale attack. If you start the conversation with guns ablazing – with an accusation or disparaging comment – you've already alienated your audience and put your partner on the defensive. If you're pissed off about your chap not doing his chores, for example, your opening gambit could be "The system for keeping the house tidy isn't working very well – could we come up with some new ideas together?" rather than the slightly less diplomatic "I'm fed up – why don't you get off your fat arse and do something around the house?" This will make your other half more inclined to listen and gives him a chance to put his feelings across and be part of the solution.

USE 'I' NOT 'YOU'

Relationship counsellors will always tell you to start sentences in an argument with 'I' not 'You'. For example, "I felt upset when you didn't call" rather than "You upset me by not calling." It might seem like a small matter of semantics but this natty technique stops statements sounding so accusatory. By using the word 'I' you draw attention to the way his behaviour made you *feel* rather than announcing the statement as if it were a concrete fact. The implication is that the behaviour is the problem, not the person.

To make an effective 'I' statement you need to do three things. First, you need to describe the behaviour that is bothering you. Be careful not to apportion blame. For example, "I don't like finding out that the mortgage hasn't been paid." Second, explain how the behaviour makes you feel. For example, "This really worries me because I don't want us to get a bad credit rating." And finally, make the consequences clear and suggest a way you can cooperate on moving forward. For example, "If we get a bad credit rating it could affect lots of different aspects of our life together. Why don't we set up a joint account and start a standing order?" This approach may feel a bit stilted at first, especially if you feel like ripping his head off, but it gives you a way of negotiating a potentially explosive situation and coming up with a solution that doesn't leave one partner feeling got at.

SHUT YOUR CAKE HOLE

We love the sound of our own voices don't we? Especially when we're on a roll. And yet listening, rather than talking, is the key to getting what you want. We often assume that we know what our partner is thinking or feeling. It can come as a real punch to the stomach to find out that your other half is just as unhappy about something you're doing (or not doing).

It's absolutely vital to spend at least 50 per cent of any argument listening to what your partner has to say and, if you can keep your cool, responding to their ideas in a loving, sensitive way. In Chapter 5 we looked at the importance of respect in a relationship – in particular how that means taking on board someone else's point of view, even if it doesn't tally with your own. By being understanding and empathetic, you're much more likely to get the same courtesy in return, which ultimately means finding a solution which works for *both* of you.

A really useful skill to have is something called *reflective listening*. Developed as a technique for improving communication between psychotherapists and their clients, reflective listening involves trying to understand the central idea behind what a person is saying and then repeating it back to them to confirm that you've understood them properly. Leather couch is optional.

Let me give you an example. Your partner is frustrated about the fact that you and he haven't seen much of each other lately. Listen to him fully and then paraphrase what he said in the form of a question. For example, you say, "So, you feel like we don't spend enough time together?" This gives both of you a chance to agree what the problem is, so you're not talking at cross-purposes.

The next step is to listen for his underlying emotions. This takes practice and involves putting yourself in his shoes.

For example, your partner may sound really angry but what he's actually feeling is rejection. Offer a gentle suggestion such as "You sound upset" to see if you've hit the right note. It may take a few stabs before you get to the crux of the issue.

During the conversation it's also important that your partner knows he's got your attention. Keep eye contact and avoid aggressive body language such as crossing your arms or standing over your partner. Give positive signals such as nodding your head or encouraging him to keep talking. Above all, don't try to engineer a solution on his behalf or offer your opinion unless asked for. Assume that your partner has the intelligence to come up with a solution. Ask questions such as "What do you think it would take to make this problem better?" to find out what he'd like to do.

TAKE DEEP BREATHS

Criticism is hard to hear. Especially if there's a grain of truth in it. Flying off the handle, however, is almost always counter-productive so if you feel yourself about to lose control, it's time to take some deep breaths. Not only does this focus your attention away from getting mad but it actually has a physiological effect on your body. When you start to get angry your breathing often switches to short, rapid breaths. This can raise your heart rate and blood pressure, making you feel more stressed and angry.

Criticism is hard to hear. Especially if there's a grain of truth in it.

By practising controlled deep breathing, you can keep a lid on this escalating anger, allowing you to keep calm and keep talking. When you feel yourself getting riled, simply breathe in for five counts, hold for two counts and then breathe out for five counts. (It might be worth explaining to your partner what you are doing so he doesn't think you are having some kind of asthmatic episode or doing it for dramatic effect.)

If deep breaths aren't working, you need to take a time-out. This involves moving yourself bodily away from the argument, so you can both calm down and restart the conversation later. It's important that both of you know about time-outs, so one person doesn't feel like they're being abandoned or ignored. When you feel things getting heated, you need to announce that you'd like to take a time-out. Tell your other half how long you need and where you're going (e.g. "I'm going for a quick walk to clear my head, I'll be back in 30 minutes") so they don't worry about where you've gone or that the argument is never going to get resolved. If possible, work off your anger with exercise or do something relaxing so that you return to the discussion in a better frame of mind. Whatever you do, don't get behind the wheel of a car, go down the pub to get smashed or ring your ex. All three could have dire consequences.

• • •

Changing your arguing technique may freak your partner out initially, especially if you sound too much like a therapist. It's also important that, eventually, *both* of you use healthy arguing techniques for future disagreements, not just you. Leading by example is certainly one way of achieving this –

your partner may simply copy your style if he sees it working. But chances are you'll need to explain what you're doing and why you're doing it, and suggest that he try some of these techniques in the future. He might be resistant at first, but hopefully the results will speak for themselves. If things have got really bad, an anger management course or a spell with a couples' counsellor will give both of you the tools to move forward.

. . .

7

Chapter Seven

WHAT MAKES PRINCE CHARMING COMMIT?

...

Spend a happy half-hour in the self-help section of a bookshop and you'd be forgiven for thinking that men find the idea of commitment about as appetising as a turd on a waterbiscuit. Just look at the titles: *Why Men Love Bitches; The Game; Why Men Don't Commit;* and the heart-warming *How to Be the Bad Boy Women Love: Getting Hot Women to Pursue You by Being a 'Hard to Get' Man.* Makes you want to fling yourself off a bridge.

While these books are a gripping read and sell in their millions, I'm not sure they present an entirely accurate picture of the male species. Most men do want to settle down. They do want commitment. It's just that princes might not talk about it in the same way as princesses. As American screenwriter Tad Safran wittily noted in a recent piece he wrote for *The Times*:

> "Men don't like to admit it, but we talk about relationships every bit as much as women. Especially as we get older. We don't discuss them like women do: with wisdom and familiarity. Men discuss relationships like monkeys trying to decipher sheet music. One of the main themes of our analysis is: how do you know if she's The One?"

It warms the cockles to think that blokes and commitment aren't complete strangers. Otherwise you might just as well throw in the towel now. But how can you tell if your prince is committed to the relationship and are there any ways to nudge this process along? Is timing a factor or will True Love conquer all?

• IN FOR A PENNY, IN FOR A POUND? •

Isn't it funny that, when trying to establish whether your bloke is ready for commitment, you ask everyone but him? You talk to your best friend. You drop hints to his mates. You pour over your (and his) horoscope. I've even been known have a lengthy conversation with my cat about what he thought. Not much, as it turned out. It seems the allure of cleaning his own testicles was far more interesting than solving my relationship dilemma.

Anyway, the point is that if you're truly thinking about long-term commitment with someone, surely you know each other well enough to have a frank conversation about it? It's amazing how many women worry about bringing up the subject with their other half. What if I scare him off? What if he thinks I'm pushing him? What if he's not ready and I ruin the relationship just by talking about the future?

Come on. Get real. If your bloke is too immature to have an adult conversation about the future, do you really think he's ready to skip down the aisle? If he blanches at the prospect of a 'where are we going' conversation, I suspect the likely answer is 'nowhere'. Being committed to someone involves being open and honest about the relationship. Coyness and commitment don't sit well together.

And anyway, what if he's just waiting for you to show him *you* are ready? You've got to feel sorry for poor old Prince Charming. It's still usually the case that we expect *him* to take the initiative and ask us to use a drawer, move in, get married or whatever the next step is. You can't blame him for being worried that you might say no.

I'm not saying that you should bombard your bloke with a 10-year plan, especially if you've only been together for a few months. Anyone is going to panic if they feel that their life has been mapped out by someone else. There has to be a sense that you are both building a future *together* rather than you presenting him with a timetabled fait accompli. (If you don't believe me, leave a few copies of *Mother & Baby* magazine around the house or constantly hum the Wedding March – risky, but great fun.) Giving ultimatums rarely works either – if you've had to resort to bribery, I suspect the relationship isn't as brilliant as you first thought.

> There has to be a sense that you are both building a future *together* rather than you presenting him with a timetabled fait accompli.

The best way to approach conversations about commitment is to keep things relaxed, fairly brief and non-pressured. A bloke will feel much less frightened by open-ended questions such as "What do you feel about marriage?" rather than "When are we going to get married?" Further down the line, when you feel more confident about his level of commitment, the conversations will need to become more specific and the plans more concrete. But don't run before you can walk.

Both of you can test your commitment by looking at the following ten statements to see how relevant they feel. Once you've had a chance to mull these over, it's then time to talk to your partner about the implications for your relationship:

1 My partner makes me happy.

2 I'm with my partner because I *want* to be and not because I have to be.

3 I hate the idea of us splitting up.

4 I hate the idea of starting a new relationship.

5 I'm happy to know that this relationship will take hard work and compromise if it's going to last the distance.

6 I'm optimistic and excited about building a life with my partner.

7 We share the same hopes and aspirations for the future.

8 I want to be with my partner for as long as possible.

9 We have the same views about marriage

10 We have the same views about whether we want kids or not.

Is there anything you can do to encourage a prince to commit? Perhaps. (We'll look at those things in a minute.) But what is certain is that there are lots of things you shouldn't do to coerce someone into a long-term relationship. Love should be given freely, not because you're holding a metaphorical gun to his head.

• FIVE WAYS *NOT* TO GET HIM TO • COMMIT

1 **Get pregnant.** This has to be one of the craziest attempts to get someone to stay. Not only is it totally unfair to him, it's an unforgivable thing to do to your child. You're also shooting yourself in the foot. Yes, he

might stay, but do you really want someone who's only with you because they feel guilty? And, if he doesn't stay – and who can blame him – you're left with the unenviable task of raising a child by yourself. (Speaking as someone who was a single mum for different reasons – I can say with absolute conviction that it's the toughest job in the world ... ever.)

2 **Jealousy.** Going for the "I'll soon make him realise what he's missing" approach is another risky strategy. By flirting outrageously with anything in trousers, you might succeed in making him jealous but what happens when you stop? If he only wants you when he thinks he might lose you, how can you ever have a normal relationship? If you are in this situation watch out, you might be dating Mr Player (see Chapter 1) and he's only interested in the thrill of the chase, not you.

3 **Making it financially difficult for him to extricate himself.** You can feel him slipping away. Your relationship is on the rocks. Here's a good idea. Why not buy a flat together? Start a business? Invest all your joint savings in a crumbling farmhouse? No no no. By lashing yourself together financially, you've not in any way dealt with the underlying problems in the relationship – in fact, you've probably hastened its demise. Financial stress is one of the quickest ways to end a beautiful relationship and will never rescue a failing one. It also makes splitting up much more painful, messy and, if solicitors have to get involved, costly.

4 **Total dependency.** But you can't leave me, I've got nowhere to go! Making yourself totally dependent on someone financially or emotionally is no guarantee against the relationship ending. This is the 21st century. Women are expected to stand on their own two feet, not hang onto the coat-tails of a paternalistic boyfriend. In fact, your dependency may have been endearing to begin with, but it's probably starting to get right up your boyfriend's nose. Since when was a relationship a free meal ticket?

5 **Making yourself indispensable.** You also can't ingratiate your way into someone's heart. You might think that making yourself indispensible is a guarantee against being humped and dumped but don't you believe it. The more socks you pick up or debts of his you pay, the less likely he is to treat you with the respect you deserve. Relationships need to be on an equal footing – it's lovely to make your partner a cup of tea now and again, just make sure you don't become an unpaid butler, barmaid and bankroller all in one.

Financial stress is one of the quickest ways to end a beautiful relationship and will never rescue a failing one.

• TEN WAYS TO HELP HIM COMMIT •

While it's pointless trying to make someone commit, there are things you can do to build commitment in a relationship. None of these involves trapping or tricking your partner. The following suggestions can help make your relationship stronger and more enjoyable so that both of you feel like moving on to the next stage.

1 **Learn to argue.** How does the saying go? "Give me strength to change the things I can, courage to accept the things I can't, and wisdom to know the difference." Couples who learn to accept and celebrate their differences will find it easier to make long-term commitment work. Follow the steps in Chapter 6 to make sure that you learn how to deal with disagreement in a way that leaves you both feeling valued and listened to.

2 **Make time for intimacy.** We already know that a loving and active sex life is a fantastic way to deepen the bond between you both. If your bedroom has become a battleground or barren desert, take time to reignite your relationship. If you're stuck for ideas, there are lots of helpful books, internet advice sites or DVDs you can look at together. If the problem goes deeper, a sympathetic GP or relationship counsellor will soon get to the bottom of it.

3 **Give him space.** The more anxious you feel about a partner, the tighter you tend to hold the reins. No-one likes being controlled and the more you grip, the more he'll want to buck or pull away. Whoa there me beauty! Demonstrate that you trust him, love him and feel secure in the relationship by letting him have his own space, time, friends and interests. Absence definitely makes the heart grow fonder (unless, of course, his idea of freedom involves spending a week in Las Vegas tucking dollar

bills into a lapdancer's thong, in which case forget it and forget him).

4   **Find things in common.** I draw the line at His and Hers dressing gowns but by all means find hobbies or interests you can enjoy together. Couples who play together stay together, although perhaps it might be wise to avoid super-competitive sports such as squash or singles tennis, where he'll take great pleasure in grinding you to a pulp, or pursuits where your skill levels are wildly mismatched. (The last time my husband, who's dyslexic, played me at Scrabble, for example, we almost ended up in separate bedrooms. Sore loser in my opinion.)

5   **Spend time with couples.** Men often fear commitment if they've spent too much time around couples who constantly bicker or young parents with devil-like children. Why would marriage seem appealing if all you've got to look forward to is years of sniping at each other and snivelling brats? Spend time with couples who've made a success of commitment and families who blatantly enjoy each other's company. Never underestimate the power of positive role models.

6   **Tell him you love him.** That's enough about you, let's talk about me. Women often spend a disproportionate amount of a relationship seeking reassurance rather than offering it. While you don't need to tell your bloke you love him 20 times a day – that may be interpreted as a touch needy – there's certainly no harm in reminding

him how much he means to you. It's also important for him to know that you love him for the person he is, not for his bank balance, job title or earning potential.

7 **Be yourself.** In the first few months of a relationship, it's difficult not to put on an act. You're trying to make a good impression and that's completely understandable. But spending the rest of your life being someone you're not is a recipe for disaster. It also makes it difficult for your partner to commit because he may have a sneaking suspicion that he's not getting the full picture. Be yourself and it will encourage him to be the same.

8 **Enjoy his friends and family.** You won't like all your bloke's friends. In fact, some of them are probably complete dicks. Same goes for his family. But that doesn't mean you shouldn't try and make an effort to be polite. They say that you should judge a person by his choice of friends. If you think his entire friendship group are insufferable, it might be time to wonder whether you and your partner have got as much in common as you thought you had. Family is even more important. Blood is thicker than water, so you're going to struggle if you insist on making him choose between you and his close relatives.

9 **Be independent.** Ask most blokes and they'll tell you that there's nothing sexier than a woman who's independent. The best relationships are those where both parties are allowed to operate as individuals within

the framework of being a couple. You're together because you want to be, not because you can't survive apart. Any bloke worth his salt will love the fact that you both bring different things to the table. If you have your own career, interests and opinions, it's much easier to keep your relationship fresh and exciting in the long run. There's nothing more depressing than those couples in restaurants who sit in silence and stare into the distance because they ran out of things to say to each other 10 years ago.

10 **Dream big.** I'm sure that some blokes shy away from commitment because they think it spells the end of ambition and aspiration. Nothing could be further from the truth. Being in a couple is exciting. The future should be full of possibilities and adventures. Make it clear that together you are invincible. Together you're going to do things that you could never dream of doing separately. Together you're going to give each other the courage to take risks and achieve great goals. You're going to be the wind under each other's wings. (I'm quoting Bette Midler – it must be time for my medication.)

Ask most blokes and they'll tell you that there's nothing sexier than a woman who's independent.

• DO MEN HAVE A BIOLOGICAL •
CLOCK?

We women know a thing or two about timing. Most of us feel our biological clocks ticking quietly away and have a general idea about when we think it's the right time to settle down and start a family. A woman's fertility doesn't last forever and we have a finite period in which to find someone we like enough to start a family with, if that's what we want. The advent of IVF has meant that some women have been able to extend their fertility well into their fifties but anyone who's undergone fertility treatment will know how tortuous the process is. On top of that, most specialists refuse to give IVF treatment to women beyond their early forties, so the reality is that we've only given ourselves an extra decade or so to find someone we want to raise children with (unless you want to go it alone, of course).

Guys have it somewhat easier. Although the quality of a man's sperm diminishes after he hits 40, it only takes one little swimmer to make a baby. It's not unusual for blokes to father children well into their sixties. The world's oldest new dad fathered his latest child at the tender age of 90 and apparently plans to keep extending his family for at least another decade – yikes. Without the sense of urgency that we ladies feel, does timing really matter to men? Do they hear any sort of biological ticking, however faint?

Talk to most eligible princes and you might be pleasantly surprised to hear that they do have a sense of when they'd like to settle down. While blokes in their early twenties rarely think beyond the general idea that they'd like to settle down at some stage in the distant future, most guys in their late twenties and early thirties are starting to take the idea more seriously. In fact, 'when' seems to become almost as important as 'who'.

Remember Tad Safran from the beginning of the chapter? He describes this idea as the 'New York Taxi Driver theory' – it's a touch cynical but it nicely illustrates the point:

> "According to this idea, men – like New York taxi drivers – cruise around all day, picking up fares. They carry some for a long time, some for just a short while, without giving it all that much thought. But at a certain point, when they're tired, maybe bored and have had their fill, the taxi driver decides it's time to turn off his light and go home. Whoever is in the back of his metaphorical relationship taxi at that point is the one he marries. The clever women are the ones who quietly cling on in there, monopolising the back seat, with the doors firmly locked, until the driver is ready to turn off his meter."

I'm not sure it's as unromantic as that; nor that you should doggedly cling on for years to land someone who may turn out to be Mr Wrong. But there's a grain of truth in the idea that timing is very important to *both* sexes, especially in a climate when other factors such as career, money and stability exert such a powerful force. There's a huge pressure on both men and women to carve a professional life out for themselves before they settle down, as well as a cultural assumption that we should have had a generous (but not too generous) sprinkling of relationships before we tie ourselves to one person. Despite the fact that men can, biologically, father children well into their twilight years, there's an unwritten rule that leaving it too late is a bit naff. Men do have a biological clock. Not only does their fertility slow down as they get older, although not to the same extent as women's, but the physical demands of looking after small children require you to be fairly spritely. I think most men are aware of this, and it may play a part in their decision-making process.

So where does that leave your prince and whether he's ready to commit? I suppose what I'm saying is that there are:

- plenty of things you can do which *won't* help your prince commit

- an even greater amount of things you *can* do to strengthen your relationship and thereby encourage your prince to feel more committed

- certain factors, including timing, which might help or hinder this process along.

That's not to say that if you meet the man of your dreams when you are both 17 that you're not destined to be together. It's just that most men are probably working along the principle of right princess, right time. In fact, if we're honest with ourselves, so are most women.

• • •

8

Chapter Eight

LIVING HAPPILY EVER AFTER . . .

...

If you believe in fairytales, kissing frogs is actually a good thing. In the children's story, the princess is initially very reluctant to pucker up. In fact, she does everything in her power to avoid her slimy suitor. She finally relents, however, only to be rewarded by the transformation of her amphibious lover into a strapping 6-foot prince. Three cheers for going against your better judgement.

It's amazing how potent this fairytale is. Who amongst us hasn't, at some stage, persisted with an unpromising partner in the hope that one day he'll change into something magical? You convince yourself that if you love him and kiss him enough, the spell will be broken and he'll turn into the prince you've always dreamed of. Sadly, unlike the fairytale, in reality it seems that it's invariably a case of 'once a frog always a frog'.

But here's something interesting. In early versions of this Brothers Grimm fairytale, the princess doesn't actually kiss the frog. While he's desperately trying to coerce her into some froggy action, she's having none of it. He even tries to trick his way into her bed; "I am tired," moans the frog, "I want to sleep as well as thou, lift me up or I will tell thy father." But instead of acquiescing, the princess grows furious, picks up the frog by his legs and flings him against the wall with all her might. "Now, thou wilt be quiet, odious frog," she quips.

Splat. I much prefer that ending. Messy but very satisfying. It also neatly ties up what I hope you've gleaned from this book – that kissing frogs is absolutely no strategy for a finding a prince. If nothing else, I hope it's left you better equipped to spot a frog at fifty paces. And, even if you date one by mistake, this book should help you recognise the warning signs before he hops off and breaks your heart.

With any luck you'll have also gained insight into why we make the choices we do, why we go for particular types of men, and what we can do to break those patterns. We've learned about common mistakes women make in relationships, why we make them without even knowing it and why they are so deadly for a relationship. Above all, I want you to take away with you a sense of what a healthy, happy relationship should feel like and what kinds of traits make a prince truly charming.

But what happens *after* you've fallen into each other's arms and floated off into the sunset? Is it going to be plain sailing from now on? Don't you believe it. Finding your prince is just the beginning of the adventure – now things start to get *really* interesting ...

• WHEN THE CHIPS ARE DOWN •

Love is easy when life is breezy. How difficult is it to be cheerful when you're metaphorically skipping through meadows? Relationships should have more than their fair share of high days and holidays and it's vital that you make the most of the good times.

But, however blissful the relationship, you'll can't avoid the inevitable crises and calamities that befall us all. Life is all about change – some good, some bad. You can't go round it. You have to go through it. Some change is exciting – having a baby or coming into money. Some change is excruciating – the death of a loved one or losing a job. Either way, it can pull the rug from under your relationship.

What separates couples who stay the distance from those who fall apart is how well they deal with change. Those people who embrace change seem to fare better than those who fight it. And whether it's a windfall or a wake-up call, the better prepared you are, the greater the chance you'll come out the other side a stronger and more stable couple.

> Life is all about change – some good, some bad. You can't go round it. You have to go through it.

• HOW DO YOU DEAL WITH CHANGE? •

Before we look at the right way to deal with change, let's take a quick look at some unhelpful strategies that we often resort to if we're faced with a new set of circumstances:

- **The Emu** – Rather than look change in the eye, you prefer to bury your head in the sand and hope that it will go away. You find it difficult to adjust to new situations and prefer to plough ahead regardless, ignore the signs, or block out your feelings with drink, drugs or some other distraction. You might as well just stick your fingers in your ears and say "La la la la la it's not happening ..."

- **The Dreamer** – Life was always better in the past. You spend most of your time wishing things were the way they were, rather than the way they are now. You can't accept that change is inevitable and prefer to find solace in nostalgia and 'what ifs'. You feel you have little control over what happens in your life – you are simply a cork bobbing along in the sea.

- **The Change Junkie** – You revel in change. In fact, you love change too much. You feel bored if things stay the same for too long and routine makes you uneasy. Even if you've found something or someone that makes you happy, you feel it can't last. You actively seek out change and may even upset the apple cart simply for something to do.

None of these strategies is going to help a relationship. All change, whether good or bad, brings with it a sense of uncertainty and anxiety. Some changes are also hugely exciting. As a couple, you can help each other through change by:

(a) learning to handle change better as an individual

(b) adopting strategies for dealing with change as a couple.

• HELPING YOURSELF THROUGH • CHANGE

- **Don't be too hard on yourself.** Change is traumatic, however exciting on the face of it. We've all seen the trail of devastation a big lottery win can bring, let alone a small baby, so it's no surprise that any kind of change, good or bad, is going to stir up some difficult emotions. Don't be surprised if you find yourself laughing one minute and weeping the next.

- **Cry if you want to.** Change inevitably means letting go. Even if you've longed for a new job or couldn't wait to get divorced, don't be surprised if you still find yourself grieving for your past life. It doesn't mean you shouldn't have changed – it just means that you've rightly acknowledged that things are going to be different from now on.

- **Resistance is futile.** Ignoring or railing against change will only make things harder in the long run. Denial is emotionally draining and will use up any energy that you need to make decisions about how to make the most of your new situation.

- **Bitch about it.** Don't deal with things by yourself. Your partner will be a great source of support, but it's also important to look outside your relationship and seek different points of view from friends, family and professionals. Get things off your chest – you'll feel a million times better.

- **Divide and conquer.** Don't look at change as one big scary thing. Break it down into its constituent parts and deal with each problem on its own merits. For example, changing jobs may involve reorganising finances, moving house, changing childcare arrangements, as well as getting your head around your new role. Looking at all these changes as small steps will stop you feeling overwhelmed and help you to tackle each one in turn.

- **Chin up.** There are always tiny glimmers of hope even in the darkest of situations. People who survive deeply traumatic life-changing events are those who feel they can pluck something positive out of the experience. Even if you simply come out the other side a stronger, more thoughtful person, that's still something to be proud of.

• HELPING EACH OTHER THROUGH • CHANGE

- **Make time.** Try to make more time for each other if you know that a period of change is about to happen. Whether you turn off the TV or leave work a bit earlier, it'll really help if you set aside a few extra hours to talk things through together or make a plan of action.

- **Be honest.** Don't ignore the subject in the hope that it will go away. Chat about what the change will mean for you as a couple and as individuals. Express your hopes and fears openly and come up with some practical ideas for reducing the stress.

- **Acknowledge each other's fears.** You might not be worried, but what if your partner is? Be sympathetic to his anxieties and allow him time and space to work through them. Some people fear change because they have had difficult experiences of transition in the past – take those feelings into account.

- **Involve each other in decisions.** You might be the one changing track, but it will affect both of you as a couple. Make decisions about change as a partnership and try to accommodate each other's wishes.

- **Mark the change.** Do something which celebrates or honours the change, even if it's a difficult time.

- **Keep life as normal as possible.** Change doesn't have to be overwhelming. If one of you is going through a tumultuous time, try to keep the rest of your daily routine as stable as possible.

- **Don't throw more change into the mix.** Changes are best dealt with one at a time. Don't plan to move house, for example, when you've just found out you're having your first baby.

- **Be kind to each other.** Make sure you both eat well, sleep and relax – the more rested and healthy you both feel, the less likely you are to take chunks out of each other. Give each other lots of positive encouragement and extra squeezes.

- **Laugh about it.** I'm not saying you should guffaw your way through every funeral, but if you can chuckle at life's little frustrations, you'll find it a lot easier to cope as individuals and as a couple. If it's a choice between laughing and crying, I know which one I'd choose.

• FORCING YOUR PRINCE TO CHANGE •

What happens when Prince Charming starts piling on the pounds? As he stuffs yet another chocolate éclair into his cheeks, it might take all you've got to stop yourself rugby tackling him to the ground and drop-kicking the offending confectionery into next Tuesday. This isn't what you signed up for. No-one asked you if you minded whether your partner starting chubbing out, took up chain-smoking or developed an unhealthy interest in pigeon fancying.

What happens when Prince Charming starts piling on the pounds?

So what's a princess to do? Do you have a right to change someone, even if they don't want to change? One of the biggest gripes in long-term relationships is one partner trying to change the other. Sometimes it's completely understandable that one half might want things to change, especially if a loved one has developed a bad habit or started to neglect themselves. But is it right?

The problem is that forcing someone to change is very hard and can create more problems than it solves. Left unchecked, constant sniping can cast a shadow over an entire relationship and the original issue is soon lost in a muddle of resentment and anger. Many partners simply dig their heels in, leaving the other person feeling frustrated. The more one half nags, the deeper the heels dig. What started out as an argument about one too many cream cakes soon descends into a long-running power struggle with no end in sight.

So what are your options? The first thing to say is that you should forget trying to coerce someone into changing. Threats, ultimatums, bullying, guilt-trips – they're never good ways to get what you want and you'll probably only succeed in pushing your partner away. The second thing to note is that the carrot always works better than the stick. By using lots of encouragement, praise and positive reinforcement, you might be able to tease out some changes. If you're worried about him porking out, for example, applaud any steps he takes to get more exercise, eat healthily or cut out junk food. Praise is a damned sight more effective than constant put-downs and criticism.

Above all, you have to work out what your bottom-line is. If he can't or won't change, you need to work out just how important this problem is. If his behaviour is seriously affecting your quality of life, then it's time to think about moving on. If you're just being a picky bitch, however, it's time to drop the nagging and love your partner warts and all.

• RELATIONSHIP BRICKS AND • MORTAR

Most of a relationship is made up of the mundane. Commuting to work, cooking supper, getting the car MOT'd, washing each other's clothes and so on. And while it's difficult to get all goose-pimply about scrubbing someone else's gussets, there's something deeply romantic about everyday life as a couple. When my husband and I got married I wanted to say a few words at the reception. Thinking it would be easy to come up with some devastatingly witty speech, I actually found it really difficult to say how I felt. Only when I started thinking about the things that mattered to me most about our relationship – walking the dog, putting our daughter to bed, sharing the working day's events over a glass of wine – did I realise that the litmus test of love is to find pleasure in everyday life.

The devil's in the detail, not in the occasional grand gesture.

Once you have that happy foundation, you can embellish your relationship with all sorts of sparkles and twiddly bits. A solid footing will allow you both to be more adventurous as a couple, try new things and take more risks. You'll struggle to have a rich and fulfilling sex life, for example, if one of you is pissed off because the washing up hasn't been done or the gas bill remains unpaid. The devil's in the detail, not in the occasional grand gesture.

• KEEPING ON BUILDING •

The surest way to live 'happy ever after' is to be alive to your relationship and work at it. People often get disheartened if suddenly a relationship becomes hard work. But there's a clear distinction to make here. Loving someone shouldn't be hard work. If you have to force yourself to have feelings for a partner, you're with the wrong guy. But that's absolutely *not* the same as saying that a relationship shouldn't involve hard work. In the same way that you'd put lots of effort and energy into a rewarding career, your relationship deserves as much attention and elbow grease. Nothing that's worth having is easy. The great thing about working at a relationship, however, is that it's often hugely enjoyable. The following five ways to build your relationship, for example, are far more fun than you'd ever have in the office ...

1 **Be mates.** You might fancy the pants off each other but every relationship should be underpinned by a great friendship. Your partner should also be your best friend and, as such, deserves the same closeness, respect and honesty that your girlfriends get. Do what friends do – laugh, share, gossip, play. You never know, he might let you paint his toenails if you ask nicely.

2 **Put your relationship first.** When work's tough or you start a family, it can be easy to put your relationship on the back burner. Don't. Your stability as a couple is what gives you the energy to tackle the rest of your life and makes for a happy home environment. Protect the bond between you two rather than putting it last. Set aside quality time to spend as a couple – aim for at least 15

minutes of uninterrupted conversation a day and try to steal half a day for a hot date at least once a fortnight.

3   **Touch each other.** Whether it's a quick hug or a furious humping, physical intimacy is important for your relationship. The daily grind of life can leave your libido lacking but it's vital to communicate your love for your partner. It doesn't have to be passionate – hugs, kisses and cuddles are just as important as chandelier swinging – but if your sex-life takes a nosedive, it can be a sign of underlying problems or unexpressed anger. Deal with these feelings, either through talking to each other or to a third party, and the intimacy should return in no time.

4   **Get out the fizzy pop.** If you're making a success of your relationship, celebrate it. Find any reason to congratulate yourself as a couple – whether it's surviving your first row or celebrating 50 years of wedded bliss. Make a big deal of anniversaries, birthdays and other special markers. Crack open the champagne and surprise each other with thoughtful gifts. Remind each other of all the things you've achieved together and be generous with your compliments.

> If you're making a success of your relationship, celebrate it.

5   **Enjoy the good times.** When your relationship is blossoming, take the time to identify the things that make it so good. Are things great because you've been spending more time together? Have you been making any special

efforts recently? Is your partner responding to some positive changes that you've made? The more you understand what makes your relationship tick, the more able you'll be to create lots of happy times together.

A relationship should be something that brings you more happiness than heartache. It sounds blindingly obvious but it's amazing how fraught romance can get. I've been in long-term relationships where the ratio of good times to bad times was probably no better than 50:50. What's even more crazy is that I stuck at these love affairs for months, even *years* sometimes, knowing that they were doing me no good.

Life, thankfully, isn't like that now. But it's taken a while to get there. What's striking is that being in a great relationship doesn't feel odd. After such a long time dating arseholes, surely it should feel unnerving to be with someone who isn't putting me down or playing games? But it's not. And, if I think about why, it's because deep down in the dark recesses of my mind I always knew what a good relationship would feel like. I think most of us have actually got a good instinct about what makes us happy. The problem is that we stop listening to our gut and instead get side-tracked.

Don't give up on finding your Prince Charming – he's out there.

If this book does only one thing, I hope that it encourages you to believe that there is such a thing as happy ever after. Crap relationships are draining. Good ones fill you full of hope and ambition. Don't give up on finding your Prince Charming –

he's out there. You simply need to stop getting distracted by frogs and start believing you actually have a right to be in a supportive, fun-packed and loving relationship. Now that's what I call a fairytale ending ...

• • •

More titles from *Prentice Hall Life*, so you can learn today how to change your life for a better tomorrow ...

Annie Lionnet

brilliant

Relationships

Your ultimate guide to attracting and keeping the perfect partner

ISBN 9780273718338

Read on for an extract ...

CHAPTER 5

Choose your perfect match

'Love alone can unite living beings so as to complete and fulfil them ... for it alone joins them by what is deepest in themselves'.
Pierre Teilhard de Chardin, theologian and philosopher

Trust your intuition

Have you ever failed to follow your intuition or repressed your instincts about somebody only to realise later that you should have paid more attention? One of your best allies in knowing if you are making the right choices is your own inner knowingness. Just think about it. The moment you meet someone, there is usually a voice within that tells you if that person is someone you can trust, connect and feel safe with. So why don't we always listen to it? Well, when it comes to romantic love, sexual chemistry and our emotions are usually much louder and more urgent and may drown our inner voice out. But if you are serious about finding your perfect match, it's imperative that you listen to the messages that your inner voice is telling you. No matter how out of practice you are at tuning into and following your inner knowing, your intuition will always guide you in the right direction if you listen to it.

> Your intuition will always guide you in the right direction if you listen to it

Learning to listen to this inner compass is essential to attracting what will fulfil and nurture you on all levels. So what is that knowingness? People experience it in different ways, but you could say first and foremost that it is a feeling. Your feelings about someone, any insights you have, intuition, deep certainties, are messages from your inner knowing. They come before you have time to rationalise. Knowingness is simply a gut feeling.

Turn the page for more ...

Enhance your ability to attract a partner

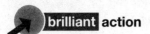 **brilliant** action

Take a look at the list below and see how many statements ring true for you.

- I want but don't need to be in a relationship.
- I live in accord with my needs and values.
- I have healthy self esteem and I know my worth.
- I keep my life in balance.
- I have a good circle of friends.
- I enjoy my work.
- I see romance and sex as part of a relationship, not the whole relationship.
- I am realistic about the kind of relationship I want.
- I am confident that I will choose someone who is the best for me.

If you agreed with all or most of these statements it's highly likely that you are happy with yourself and your life and attracting your perfect match would simply serve to double your happiness.

Being happy with yourself makes you much more magnetic to others. In fact, often we attract the best partners when we are neither looking for nor avoiding the possibility of finding someone.

Living your life to the full whilst being completely open to meeting someone is a powerful combination. After all, the key to your happiness and the quality of your relationships ultimately depends on your ability to be comfortable and content with who you are. When you acknowledge and appreciate your inherent worth you invite others to do the same. In other words, live your best life and you will attract your best partner...

If life is what you make it, then making it better starts here.

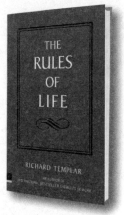

9780273706250

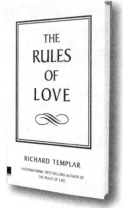

9780273720256

9780273725527

9780273716983

9780273718338

Prentice Hall Life books help you to make a change for the better. Together with our authors we share a commitment to bring you the brightest ideas to manage your life, work and wealth.

In these books we hope you'll find the ideas you need for the life you want. Go on, help yourself.

It's what you make it.